Beauties of
IRAN

Photos
S.Mahmoudi Aznaveh

Text
M.T.Faramarzi

To my wife
Shiva Khoshnevis

S. Mahmoudi Aznaveh

محمودی ازناوه، سعید، ۱۳٤٦-
زیبایی های ایران/ عکس های سـعید محمـودی ازنـاوه؛
متن محمد تقی فرامرزی.- تهران: یساولی، ۱۳۷۹.
۲٤٤ ص. : مصور.
ISBN 964-306-054-3
فهرستنویسی بر اساس اطلاعات فیپا.

۱. عکسها- - ایران. الف. فرامرزی، محمد تقـی، ۱۳۲۵-
، مترجم. ب. عنوان.

۷۷۹/۹۰۰	TR ٦٥٤/م۳ز۹
[۹۰۰/۰۰۲۲۲]	[DSR ۷۸]
۷۹-۷٦۸۰ م	کتابخانه ملی ایران

Beauties of Iran
Photographer: S. Mahmoudi Aznaveh
Text: M.T. Faramarzi
Designed by: J. Yassavoli
Colour Separation: Farayand-e Gouya
Lithography: Naqshafarin.
First edition: 2001
Cover design: R. Yassavoli
Print House: Soroush
Printed and bound in the Islamic Republic of Iran
Published and distributed by Yassavoli Publications
Bazaarcheh Ketab, Enqelab Ave. 13146, Tehran, Iran.
Tel: (9821) 6461003 Fax: (9821) 6411913
web site: www.yassavoliran.com

ISBN 964-306-054-3

CONTENTS

Sa'eed Mahmoodi Aznaveh is a historic relics restoration graduate deeply attached to the ancient architecture of this land. In his early youth, he forwent playing with toys befitting his age, spending his meager resources on buying photographic equipment and films. In those years, photography gradually became his main hobby.

His infatuation with the culture and civilization deeply rooted in this country's popular traditions, historic relics and Islamic architecture caused his photographs to transcend the mere recording of subjects within bounded frames, achieving a particularly profound expression. We accompany Aznaveh's camera on a tour from the apertures of wind-towers soaring atop the desert structures to the pleasant cool atmosphere of cellars. We tread the endless meandering streets of Semnan. We cross the crowded bazaar of Kashan to reach the magnificent Emam Square in Esfahan, going on to rest in the shade of the majestic bridges of Khaju and Allahverdi-Khan spanning the Zayandeh-Rood. Therefrom we set out towards the bathhouses of Fin and Ganj-'Ali-Khan, cleansing our bodies and clothes before going on to kiss the mutilated prayer niche of the Blue Mosque of Tabriz. We then move on to Natanz, which appears as a piece of paradise fallen on the earth. The charming Shahzadeh Garden in Mahan is another stopover which leaves us with indelible memories. We continue our tour on the threshold between waking and dream. contemplating the enchanting nature of Rijab, the majestic waterfall of Bisheh, the lofty dome, of Soltaniyeh, the mausoleum of the enraptured mystic Zendeh-Pil Sheikh Ahmad-e Jam, Cheshmeh 'Ali in Damghan, the heights of Do-Hezar, the water cisterns of Na'in, Saint Stepanos church in Jolfa, the bas-reliefs of Taq-e Bostan, the rock-face inscriptions of Ganjnameh in Hamadan, the ruins of the Hundred Columns of Persepolis, the citadel of Bam, the *tekieh* of Mir-Chakhmaq, the remains of the Portuguese Fort in Hormuz Island...

With a little attention, we can see the stalactites of 'Ali-Qapu, the colorful sash windows of the Golestan Palace, the wall paintings of Chehel-Sotun and Hasht Behesht, the sun and moon patterns in the mirror-work on the ceiling of the Rakibkhaneh, the brick-work of the congregational mosque of Zavareh, the carved stucco prayer niche of Oljaitu, and thousands of carpet weaving looms in Kerman, Kashan, Tabriz, Mashhad and Esfahan, upon which famous and anonymous artists of this land have worn out their eyes and hands. Rains of love have been pouring all over this land, even its torrid deserts. The thriving and ever fresh Iranian taste, thought and art bear testimony to this claim. Sa'eed Mahmoodi Aznaveh , who has also quenched his thirst from this rain, has attempted to reflect moments of his joy. Although he – modestly – attributes these pictu
res' attractiveness to the beauty of this country's natural landscapes, minimizing his own role and that of his camera, he deserves great praise for preparing this feast; a memorable, painstakingly complied feast for keen eyes enraptured with beauty. No one knows what meandering paths he has covered to delve into memories of the past or how many hours he has spent patiently waiting to capture a shadow in the Apadana.

Mas'ud Salehi
Summer of 2000

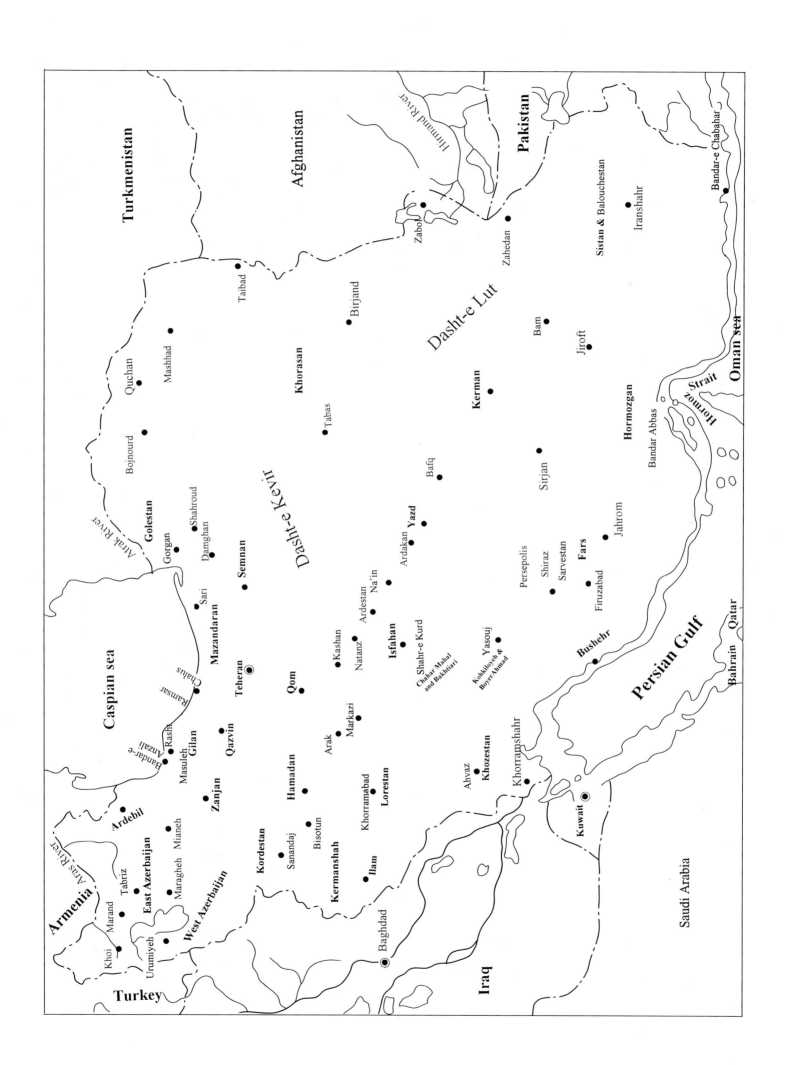

Introduction

Iran is by origin the same word as Aryan, and throughout history has been intermittently applied to the people of Indo-European, that is, Aryan origin occupying the plateau and to the plateau itself.

Today Iran is a triangle set between two depressions - the Caspian Sea to the north and the Persian Gulf to the south. It is bounded on the north by Armenia, Azerbaijan, Turkmenistan and the Caspian Sea, on the east by Afghanistan and Pakistan, on the south by the Persian Gulf and the Sea of Oman, and on the west by Iraq and Turkey.

The triangle of the Iranian Plateau is bounded by mountains rising round a central depression, a desert region formed by the bed of a dried-up ocean. The western mountains, or Zagros range, run from north-west to south-east, and the northern part of the triangle is formed by the mighty Alborz range; skirting the southern shore of the Caspian Sea, it forms a high and narrow barrier which separates the coastal area with its luxuriant vegetation from the desert regions of the interior.

In the country fringing the Alborz and Zagros ranges and in certain mountain valleys conditions for life are more favourable, owing to the better water-supply and to the fertile soil. On the higher mountains the snow falls in winter, building up a reserve of moisture for the dry summer months; there are also winter and spring rains. All the larger centres of population and the majority of the smaller ones are situated near or in the mountains because of the more abundant supplies of water that are available. These two chains, which meet in the north-west, serve as buttresses for the central plateau, a relatively arid region which varies in altitude from over 6,000 to under 2,000 feet. On this plateau the rainfall is relatively sparse, and in the lower-lying regions the soil is very saline, making cultivation, and therefore life, impossible, except in the few oases such as that of Tabas.

Two great deserts, the Dahst-e Lut and the Dasht-e Kevir, occupy a large part of the central plateau and together account for one half of the desert area and one sixth of the total area of Iran. These two deserts are often pock-marked with the round air-holes of qanats, underground channels which connect the water-table with farms and villages. They are anything up to thirty miles long, and may entail the digging of a shaft several hundred feet deep, and have been a unique Persian speciality for many centuries, and form a prodigiously complex system of water distribution.

Tehran - the capital of Iran – is located at the foothills of the Alborz mountains; the city's relatively temperate climate was the principal attraction for the Qajar monarchs. There are several royal palaces including the Sahebqaraniyeh palaces in northern Tehran, and the Golestan and Marmar (Marble) palaces in southern Tehran, now turned into museums. The Shams-ol Emareh and the Imam Mosque (formerly "Royal Mosque" or "Masjid-e Shah"), are both near the bazaar (the commercial centre).

The Alborz range covers the entire Caspian coast stretching from Khorasan in the east to northwestern Iran. Three roads lead to the Caspian provinces from Tehran, namely the Chalus, Haraz and Firuzkuh roads. The Chalus road is the most scenic route, winding its way through towns and villages towards the southern tip of the Caspian Sea. People living in these towns still wear their traditional costumes and speak their traditional dialects. A short drive from Chalus will lead to Kelardasht, one of the most attractive areas the traveller will cross on this road. Travelling inland past the provincial capital Rasht and the town of Fuman, we arrive at the growing but well –preserved village of Masouleh. The mountainside village has been declared a UNESCO World Heritage Sight, undoubtedly for its rare architecture, where houses dominate each other. As well as growing rice, the staple food product of the area, Gilan specializes in the production of tea.

At its western end, the Alborz Range reaches Iranian Azerbaijan in the centre of which lies the salt lake of Urumiyeh. This is a densely populated region, and in its fertile valleys, wheat, cotton, rice and tobacco are cultivated. It's capital is Tabriz. The heart of the city beats in the busy alleyways and stalls of the main bazaar, which the sun struggles to illuminate through openings in the ceiling. Tabriz's position in an earthquake zone and its historical vulnerability to repeated Ottoman attacks have left the city with few historical monuments of note. One of these is the 15th century 'Blue Mosque' built under the local Qara Qoyounlu rulers. Of further interest to visitors is the Il Goli pavilion, a 19th century structure built in the middle of a lake near Tabriz.

The visible remains of the ancient city of "Rey" are on the eastern fringe of Tehran. The site, at the outlet of an abundant underground layer of water, was occupied in the Neolithic Period. Excavations of the mound of Cheshmeh Ali have yielded pottery dating from the 5th millenium B.C. The best-preserved building in Rey is the so-called Tower of Toghrol Beig, a Seljuq funerary tower dated 1139-1140.

The town of Saveh, 140 km. from Tehran, was a flourishing centre with a number of libraries during the Islamic period, until destroyed by the Mongols in the 13th century. Today its large enclosed gardens and orchards (baghs) provide a variety of fruit, especially pomegranates that are greatly appreciated. Leave Tehran by the west, we reach Qazvin, a historical city founded by Sassanian king, Shapur I. The chief things of interest in Qazvin are some fairly well preserved buildings such as Sabz-e Maidan, the pavilion of Ali Qapu, the Jame' Mosque (Masjid-e Jom.'eh).

The city of Hamadan lies at the foot of the Alvand mountain. Its foundation has been attributed to the Assyrian queen Semiramis who ruled in the 10th century B.C. The modern city is built on the remains of the ancient Ecbatana (or Hegmatana) or Place of Assembly, capital of the Medes in the 7th and 6th centuries B.C. The town continued to expand and flourish under the Achaemenians and Parthians. Its importance is further confirmed by a large Achaemenian inscription known as Ganjnameh and a large stone lion. Due to the presence of the Mausoleum of Biblical Queen, who married the Achaemenian kings Artaxerxes I (486-465 B.C.) and her foster father Easter Mordecai, the city is a popular place of pilgrimage for Iranian Jews. The medieval philosopher and physician Ibn-e Sina, or Avicenna, whose writings were studied in Europe until the 19th century, rests here. Other monumental places of the city are the Alavian Tomb, the Mausoleum of Baba Taher (the Iranian poet), and the Ali Sadr cave.

The provincial capital of Kermanshah is an important agricultural centre in western Iran, and was famous in ancient times for its superb breed of horses and excellent vineyards. It is also the land of the Kords, a proud people who maintain their own language and colourful mode of dress. The relief of Darius's victory over rebels at Bisotun near the town of Kermanshah and at Taq-e Bostan, a number of reliefs have been carved out of the mountainside, and covered by a vault. Outside, Qajar kings have also been depicted enthroned, in the style of their Sassanian forbears. The Tekiyeh-e Mo'aven-ol Molk is one of Kermanshah's religious sites, providing a beautiful example of Qajar (19th century) painting and tile-work.

The southern part of the Zagros is called Lorestan. On the slopes of the now denuded mountains once stood green forests of oak, while lower down in the valleys wheat and barley are brown. Because of the heat and drought in the plains, horses and cattle must be driven to the higher pastures of Lorestan in the summer. As a result one part of the population leads a semi-nomadic existence which is quite different from that of the people settled in the towns. Part of the Mesopotamian plain to the south-west of the Zagros ranges is called Khuzestan. The frontier runs by the Shatt-ol Arab which is formed by the junction of the Tigris and the Euphrates. Thanks to the extensive irrigation, not only cereals, but more profitable crops such as cotton, rice and sugar-cane now are grown there on a large scale. Ahvaz the capital of Khuzestan, is situated in the heart of the plain and is extremely hot most of the year.

The town of Shushtar is on the right bank of the river Gargar, flanked by Dezful in the west, and by Ahvaz and the Qir Dam in the south. Shushtar was an important site under the Parthians and Sassanians, as confirmed by the considerable number of bridges and fire temples remaining. The town's ancient water mills are among its attractions.

About 85 km. from Ahvaz a road on the left leads to the site of Susa (Shus). What is now just sand and desert - with some ancient remains brought to light by the excavators - used to be one of the most flourishing and most ancient cities of Iran. The ruins of Susa spread over four hills: the tell of the Acropolis - the royal city of the Elamites -, the tell of the Apadana - the site of the palace of Darius I -, the tell of the Royal town - used to be occupied by the residential districts for countries and officials -, and the tell of the craftsman's town (containing two different types of tombs). In the ruins of a 7th-century B.C. village on the banks of the Chahour is the so-called tomb of the prophet Daniel, which is greatly venerated by the Shiites. 45 km. south-east of Susa is Chogha Zanbil, a huge Ziggurat or artificial mound constructed by king Huban Untash at the city of Dur Untash about 1250 B.C. The king wanted to make this city the most important of pilgrimage in his realm.

Kashan lies 251 km. from the capital on the edge of the central desert. We should note that the civilization of Sialk, dating back to some 5000 years ago, flourished for some 3000 years near present-day Kashan. It has a number of popular historic sights, namely the Aqa Bozorg Mosque, the Madrasah-ye Soltan, the princely gardens of Fin. Two of the most famous are the Tabatabaei and Boroujerdi residences, with attractive plasterwork and painted decorations. The town of Natanz south of Kashan has an interesting 14th century mosque, as well as the mausoleum of Sheikh Abd-ol Samad located inside a former monastery (Khaneqah). Nearby, the village of Abyaneh is famous for its red soil that gives its constructions their fiery hues.

Isfahan is at a 414 km. distance from Tehran. It entered its period of glory when the Safavid monarch Shah Abbas I transferred the capital here from Qazvin, and proceeded to embellish his new capital with palaces and mosques. The Imam (Naqsh-e Jahan) Square is the largest enclosed square in the world. It is surrounded by three great Islamic monuments, namely the Imam Mosque (formerly the "Royal Mosque") the Sheikh Lotfollah Mosque and the Ali Qapu Palace. Isfahan has a considerable number of monuments whose description is beyond the scope of such introductory notes. We just mention the most famous ones such as Chahar Bagh Madrasah, Chehel Sotun Pavilion, the Shaking Minarets, and the Bridges of Shahrestna, Khwaju and See-o Se Pol.

Shiraz is the capital of Fars, and enjoys relatively temperate weather during the year. The 18th century ruler Karim Khan Zand made this his capital. The city is perhaps most famous as the resting place of the great poets Sa'di (died 1291 A.D.) and Hafez (died 1389 A.D.). This is also a city of flowers and of such famous gardens as Afifabad, Eram and Delgosha. Shiraz is also of religious importance, being the resting place of Seyyed Amir Ahmad known as Shah Cheragh, the brother of Imam Reza, the eighth Shiite Imam. One of the most charming residences here is the Qavam residence or Naranjestan, formerly home to the 19th century governor of Fars, Qavam-ol Molk Shirazi.

The province is extremely rich in archaeological remains. Persepolis (Takht-e Jamshid) the ceremonial capital of the ancient Persians is a few miles outside Shiraz. Other important sites are Pasargadae, capital and resting place of the Achaemenid monarch, Cyrus the Great (died 530 B.C.) and Naqsh-e Rostam with the four tombs of the Achaemenian kings.

The province of Yazd, to the east of Isfahan and on the western fringe of the great Lut desert, is some 667 km. from Tehran. Marco Polo visited Yazd on his way to China and called it the "good and noble city of Yazd". The town's hot desert climate has given rise to great many water cisterns and wind towers. The town presents ideal examples of desert constructions using mud and straw bricks, and wind towers that are natural air cooling systems. The town's Islamic monuments include the beautifully tiled Jame' mosque, the 11th century Mir Chakhmaq gate and square and the Seyyed Rokn-od Din mausoleum with its turquoise dome.

The province of Kerman is Iran's most southeasterly province after Sistan & Baluchestan. The city of Kerman includes several attractive 19th century sights, including the Bagh-e Shazdeh (Prince's Garden), the Ganjali Khan bath located in the Bazaar. The Ganjali Khan bath is now a museum, with wax figures set up to illustrate how the bath was used. The town of Mahan at a 42-km. distance contains the mausoleum of Shah Ne'matollah Vali, 15th century founder of the Ne'matollahi School of Sufism.

Another local attraction is the town of Bam, 210 km. south of Kerman. This is an area noted for its fruits particularly citrus fruit production. The new town of Bam is next to the old and now deserted, abandoned town. This extensive and set of mud-brick construction was a formidable defensive position in the 17th century.

Further to the southeast the country is only intermittently populated, and the desert encroaches even on some of the towns and villages still established there. These remarks, however, do not apply to Sistan, where Lake Hamun and the Helmand river provide some means of irrigation. Torrid heat regions for many months of the year in Sistan, and a hot wind is said to blow for 120 days.

The 55 km-wide strait of Hormoz is the narrow and crucial stretch of water that links the commerce of the Persian Gulf states to the open seas. The port of Bandar Abbas on the strait has been an important sight since Achaemenid times. Its territory includes the towns of Bandar Abbas, Minab, Bandar Lengeh, Jask and the islands of Qeshm and Abu Musa. The port of Bandar Lengeh (251 km. west of Bandar Abbas) is both hot and humid, with a noticeable population during the summer months.

To the east the Alborz chain forms the mountains of Khorasan, not very high, easy to cross and with exceedingly fertile valleys. Khorasan is Iran's largest province, bordering the states of Turkmenistan and Afghanistan. The most important centre in the province is the Shrine of Imam Reza, 8th Imam of the Shiites, in Mashhad. Devotees flock here form all over the country and from abroad. 24 km. west of Mashhad is the town of Tus, wherein is buried

Ferdowsi, 11th century author of the Shahnameh or 'The Book of Kings', and one of Iran's greatest poets.

Semnan is Khorasan's western neighbour, a province that is cool and temperate in the north where it reaches the Alborz mountains, and hot in the south on the desert fringe. Its four principal towns are Semnan, Shahrud and Bastam. Bastam has a number of sites including the tomb of the poet Bayazid-e Bastami, the Kashaneh tower, the 12th century Forumad mosque and the earlier Seljuq mosque.

A special feature of Iran is its diversity, something which is evident in all of the country's aspects. The diversity in geography has given rise to a diversity of vegetation and climate in the different regions of the country, and has made the land rich in produce and almost self-sufficient. There is very little vegetation in the vast desert tracts of the central plateau, except for palm trees round the oases. This is true also of the Persian Gulf area, where palm trees are found. The forests of Mazandaran and Gilan in the north, however, have oak, boxtree, fig, alder and ash, while the western mountains and areas in east Khorasan, west Kerman and Fars abound in pistachio, peanut, oak, walnut and maple. Shiraz, the capital of Fars, is of course renowned for the world's most graceful tree, the cypress.

The diversity of the population is quite evident in Iran. It is true that all the Iranians make up one nation, but ethnically speaking there are different groups: the people of Fars, the Baluchis, the Kords, the Lors, the Mazandaranis, the people of Gilan, the Turks and the Arabs. Each group speaks its own dialect or language, and has its own customs and culture. King Darius enumerates twenty-three different ethnic groups as the peoples of Achaemenian Empire. The list is headed by the Persians and the Medes; then come the people of Khuzestan and those of Armenia and Babylon and 'Parthawa' and Herat and Balkh and Sogdia and Khwarazm and the Saksas.

Long before the Romans dared to venture out of Italy, the Persians under Darius the Great ruled a kingdom that stretched form the Indus to the Nile. Over the centuries, this mighty realm became the prize of many conquerors- the Greeks, the Parthians, the Saracens, the Turks, the Mongols, the Afghans. A multitude of races, religions, and civilizations passed over its soil, all leaving indelible imprints, but in the face of these influences, the Persians had the strength not only to survive but also to absorb and adapt the foreign elements while retaining their own customs and traditions.

The third decade of the seventh century was the major turning point in Iranian history, in which the pattern of the country's religious, cultural and psychological development was determined up to the present age. For anyone wanting an insight into modern Iran, the events of this period are extremely important, immensely exciting and still rather mysterious. They were certainly totally unexpected; in 620 when Khosrow Parviz -the Sassanian king- had a twenty-year career of successful conquest behind him, no one could possibly have foreseen that within twenty-five years not merely his dynasty but the whole fabric of Iranian life would have been engulfed and overwhelmed.

During the Sassanian period, Persian architecture underwent major developments in both form and technique. New methods of vaulting, building of domes and constructing iwans came into being which influenced the architecture of both the Byzantine Empire and Islam in the centuries to come. During this period techniques of road-and bridge-building were developed which resulted in some of the most beautiful and enduring bridge forms on the East. In every way the Sassanian period marks an apogee in the history of architecture of this land of turquoise.

This heritage served as the basis upon which the spirit of Islam acted to create the remarkable architecture of Islamic Persia, and architecture which reached a plateau of perfection lasting from the eighth century to the dawn of the modern era. Benefiting from the techniques developed by the Sassanians and the spirit breathed into it by Islamic spirituality, this architecture evolved into a perfect statement of intelligibility and nobility, of order and harmony, of the wedding of utility and beauty, science and art. From this tradition have flowed such masterpieces as the early mosque of Damghan, the Seljuq and Mongol mosques of Varamin, Na'in and Isfahan, the private houses and bazaars of Kashan, the Gowharshad Mosque of Mashhad and the Sheikh Lotfollah and Royal mosques of Isfahan.

Bridges have been an outstanding feature of Iranian buildings since the earliest times: the dam and bridge attributed to Valerian at Shushtar, Shapur's Bridge at Dezful, the Pol-e Dokhtar and the Pol-e Khosrow between Andimeshk and Khorramabad, all in Khuzestan and the outstanding glories of Iranian bridge-building, the two great work which span the Zayandeh-rud at Isfahan - the Allah Verdi Khan (1629) and the Khwaju (1660). These two mighty structures are among the most impressive monuments in Isfahan, and are two of the most remarkable bridges in the world. Along with these remarkable monuments, there are substantial remains of Achaemenian and Sassanian palaces, impressive both in size and in detail, some of which, as at Persepolis, have been almost miraculously preserved. Of Seljuq and Mongol royal residences, however, all traces have disappeared; of the Great Palace at Ghazaniyeh, for instance, not even the foundations are visible. It is only from Safavid times that royal houses have survived intact. A sixteenth-century pavilion still stands in the grounds of the former royal palace at Qazvin. There is a late seventeenth-century kiosk in the lovely royal garden at Fin, above Kashan, in which a few wall paintings of the period have been preserved. The little palace at Behshahr (Ashraf) on the Caspian dates from the time of Shah Abbas. For practical purposes, Safavid palaces are confined to Isfahan: the Ali Qapu, overlooking the Maidan, which served at once as royal residence and a kind of grandstand for parades and polo matches; the Chehel Sotun behind it, covering the throne room; and the Talar-e Ashraf, a later and more modest structure in the grounds.

Although the ancient art of Persia came to an end when the Greeks conquered the Achaemenian empire and brought with them a provincial version of Hellenistic art, which for a time predominated, the great artistic tradition of the past, which had never wholly died out, experienced a revival under the native Sassanian dynasty, which ruled from the fourth to seventh centuries A.D. But conquest of the Sassanian empire by Arabs during the middle of the seventh century temporarily halted the great artistic florescence. How ever, soon Islamic rulers, Arabs, Seljuq Turks, Mongols, and Turkish Timurids became enthusiastic patrons of Persian craftsmen. Although painting and sculpture disappeared, since the Prophet had forbidden the making of human images, decorative arts again flourished. In fact, ceramics, glass, textiles, and metal work are considered among the best ever-made in Persia, outstanding both for beauty of design and excellence of workmanship.

The last truly creative, and in some ways the most remarkable, period of Persian art was that of the Safavid dynasty, which ruled Iran from 1501 to 1734 A.D. It was during this time that famous Persian carpets were produced at places like Tabriz, Herat, Isfahan, Kashan, and the Caucasus; carpets which have rightly been considered the very epitome of this art form. Ceramics continued to flourish, although they lacked some of the strength and animation of earlier Islamic pottery. And miniature painting, a new art form which had developed under the Mongols, came into full flower and had its golden age under the Timurid and Safavid rulers. Dealing with legends and history of Iran, which they portray in a very sophisticated style, Persian miniatures are a fitting climax to the ancient artistic tradition of Iran, which is one of the oldest and most remarkable in the world.

Archaeology and a wealth of objects which have been excavated from archaeological sites clearly indicate that Iran has always been populated, from the earliest times on, with inhabitants who are endowed with an advanced degree of civilization. Archaeological discoveries tell a tale of gifted and skillful craftsmen whose products travelled far and wide in the markets of the neighbouring countries, and this could not have been possible without the support of a culture and a civilization going back several millennia. This is no place for the presentation of documentary evidence to support such a claim. Suffice it to say that the objects excavated from Susa and Tepe Giyan and Ziwiyeh and Hasanlu and Marlik and Kelardasht, and from Torang Tepe and Shah Tepe and Tepe Hesar in Damghan and the ruins of Ray and the excavations of Sialk, and the artefacts discovered in Qaitariyeh in Tehran and Tal-e Iblis in Kerman and in Tal-e Bakun in Marvdasht and Tal-e Zahhak near Fasa and all the ancient objects discovered in natural cave-dwellings and in many other places, all these show a wonderful sense of design and the high level of craftsmanship that has been the characteristic of Persian art throughout the ages.

Culture thankfully rests on more than the visual arts; two pillars of Iranian civilization continue to flourish, language and religion. The modern Persian language, Farsi, is a member of the

14

Indo-European family of languages and, together with most of the tongues of India, belongs to the Aryan or Indo-Iranian branch of the family. This branch has one of the oldest literatures and has been less changed from the reconstructed mother Indo-European language than other members of the family. The two most ancient forms of Iranian language are the Old Persian of the cuneiform inscriptions of the Achaemenians, and Avestan, which is the language of the sacred book of the Zoroastrians. From this ancient stage there is a direct continuity to the Middle Persian languages of the Parthians and Sassanians. Finally we have the modern period of Persian, with remarkably little change in the language, since prose and poetry of the eleventh century A.D. can be understood with ease by any literate Iranian today.

It is hard to get back to the primitive beliefs of the Iranian. For the Avesta is a late compilation. But they seem to have advanced beyond the nature-worship of which traces are preserved in the Gathas, the oldest portion of the Avesta. Many centuries before the Christian era, Zarathustra (Zoroaster) received a revelation from his god Ahura-Mazda, this period saw the birth of "a purified worship, shorn of the blood-sacrifices which still soiled the altars of every Aryan people".

Zoroastrianism or Mazdaism went through changes of fortune. But the Achaemenians, from Darius onwards, and the Sassanians long after supported and protected it, and Ahura Mazda (Hormuzd) held an ever higher place in the Iranian faith. . If he was not the only god, he was the greatest of gods, as the King of Persia was the King of Kings, and effaced the others. He was the sky; he was light; he was symbolized by fire; but he had not, and could not have, an image. His will was for good, and men gained or lost merit according as they observed or disobeyed his law. "All the teaching of Mazdaism tends to produce .... What a beautiful Zend formula calls humaterm, hukhtem, huarestem, 'good thoughts, good words, good deeds' (Yasna, 19, 45). Whatever a man's condition may be - priest, warrior, farmer, or craftsman - this condition must be held by a pure man, whose thoughts, works, and deeds are pure. But the role of the Persians in the history of human thought was not confined to the spreading of beliefs of their own. Because they were in relations with so many peoples, and because they treated even the conquered well, they greatly contributed to the syncretic movement which prepared the way for the coming of the universal religions. As early as the Achaemenian epoch, this movement began to develop amply. From the east to the west of the Empire, cults were blended and gods allied. This process became more marked under the Sassanians. Situated in the center of the three great empires of the time, Constantinople, China, and India, the Sassanian Empire was to be for four centuries the point where the human mind exchanged ideas.

From Mazdaism other religions broke off - the worship of Mithra, the doctrine of Mani - which propagated and at the same time contaminated Iranian thought. With the onset of the Safavid dynasty (16th century), Islam became their state religion, which etymologically means surrender and obedience; the surrender of man to the laws governing the Universe and men, with the result that through this surrender he worships only the one God and obeys only His commands. The Shiite branch of Islam, refers to those who consider the succession to Mohammad, the Prophet- peace be upon him- to be the special right of the family of the Prophet and who in the field of the Islamic sciences and culture follow the school of the Household of the Prophet.

In conclusion the history of this vast and diverse land contains numerous pages each one mirroring the life of a nation that has had its brilliant days of glory and grandeur as well as its days of hardship and agony, and that continues its life with vigour and stamina. The roots of the tree of Iranian culture run so deep and are so closely integrated with Iranian soil that no passing storm will ever be able to shake it loose or erase the identity of its people.

Sonia Rezapour

Tehran

Capital and largest city of Iran and Tehran Province in an area of 600sq. km. since 200 years, is located in the northern part of the country. Tehran is Iran's administrative, economic, and cultural center as well as the major industrial and transportation center of the region. The city sits on the slopes of the Alborz Mountains at an elevation of about 1210 m., on the northwestern fringes of the Dasht-e Kevir, a desert in central Iran. Most of the growth is channeled along an east-west axis and toward the south; to the north, the city is constrained by the steep Alborz Mountains. Most commercial and government buildings are located in the center of the city. Residential structures predominate elsewhere. The climate has marked seasonal contrasts, with short springs and autumns separating cold winters and hot, dry summers.

History

Tehran is the latest and the largest capital city in the 7000-year history of Persia, as Iran was called by many people in the West before 1935. The original settlement of Tehran, north of the ancient city of Rey, may have been founded as early as the 4th century. By the early 13th century it was a small village. In 1221 invading Mongols led by Chenghis Khan destroyed Rey, but Tehran survived and grew slowly in the following centuries. During the reign of the Safavid Shah Tahmasp (1524-1576) a wall and four watchtowers were built around the city, and by the early 17th century Tehran had about 3000 houses. In the 1720s Afghan invaders attacked Tehran. The town defeated the initial Afghan force but fell to the main Afghan army and suffered tremendously under their occupation from 1723 to 1729. Nader Shah freed Tehran in 1729.

In 1788 Aqa Mohammad Khan, founder of the Qajar dynasty, made Tehran his capital, inaugurating the modern history of Tehran. At this time Tehran's population was estimated to be 15,000. Under the Qajar dynasty (1786-1925), Tehran grew in population and size, and new administrative buildings, palaces, mosques, and garrisons were constructed.

Tehran and the range of Shemiran.

In 1925 Reza Shah Pahlavi seized control of Iran and accelerated the gradual concentration of government functions and commerce in Tehran. The city walls were torn down, wide streets were cut through the old districts, and commercial strips grew along the new streets, challenging Tehran's once-dominant bazaar. A newer, wealthier section of the city developed on the north, and a distinct rift was created between modern, northern Tehran and traditional, southern Tehran. This trend continued through the rule of Mohammad Reza Shah Pahlavi, who ruled Iran from 1941 to 1979.

In 1979 Tehran was at the center of the uprisings that toppled the Shah, and the city suffered minor physical damage from the unrest. Revolutionaries held more than 50 U.S. citizens hostage in the U.S. embassy in Tehran from November 1979 until January 1981. The capital was also the target of numerous Iraqi strikes during the Iran-Iraq War (1980-1988).

Archaeological Museum

One of the most exciting discoveries in recent Iranian archaeology was this majestic statue of Darius the Great found December, 1972, inside the palace gatehouse at Shush (Susa). It is the first known large-scale statue in the round from Iran of the Achaemenian period, and shows the king dressed in the Persian manner similar to the king dressed in the Persian manner similar to the reliefs at Persepolis. Inscriptions in Egyptian hieroglyphics, Old Persian, Elamite and Akkadian identify the statue as being Darius I, and state that it was made in Egypt. The head is missing, and it remains uncertain whether the king wore an Egyptian or a Persian crown.

2- 3- Views of Tehran

4-5-National Museum of Iran (Iran-e Bastan), Tehran Museum

Darius the Great ruled from 522 to 486 B.C., and built a canal from the Nile River to the Red Sea along which this statue may have been transported on its way to Shush. Linguistic and stylistic peculiarities of the statue suggest a date for its carving during the latter part of the reign of Darius, about 490 B.C.

Golestan Palace

During the reign of the Safavid Shah Abbas I, a vast garden called Chahar Bagh (Four Gardens), a governmental residence and a Chenarestan, (a grove of plane trees), were created on the present site of the Golestan Palace and its surroundings. Then, Karim Khan Zand (1749-1779 A.D.) ordered the construction of a citadel, a rampart and a number of towers in the same area.

In the Qajar period, some royal buildings were gradually erected within the citadel; for instance, in 1813 which coincided with the fifth year of the reign of Fath Ali Shah, the eastern part of the royal garden was extended and some other palaces were built around the garden, called the Golestan Garden.

The Takht-e Marmar Edifice

The Takht-e Marmar (Marble Throne) structure was built by Karim Khan Zand between the years 1747 and 1751 A.H. that is in the first three years of his region. Aqa Mohammad Khan Qajar (1779-96 A.D.) decided to have it perfected. In (1791 A.D.), following the order of this Qajar king, a great deal of building materials, pieces of painting and decorations, belonging to the Royal Palace of Karim Khan, were removed from Shiraz to Tehran to be used in the Takht-e Marmar edifice.

Upon the orders of Fath Ali Shah Qajar, in (1806 A.D.) a big marble throne was made which is now to be found in the centre of the main iwan of the palace. The actual name of the Marble Throne is " Takht-e Solaimani". All around the iwan, there remain lots of paintings and decorations belonging to the Qajar period. After Fath Ali Shah's death, the other Qajar kings followed the example of their ancestors in perfecting the decorations and adorning the buildings of the Palace.

Mount Damavand

Mount Damavand, the highest mountain in Iran, has for centuries attracted mountaineers, nomads and legends to its snow-covered slopes. The epic hero Fereidun wrestled and defeated the evil giant Zahhak, chaining him to a cave on the mountain peak. Villagers living near the base of the volcano still remark that Zahhak is straining to be free at the first signs of smoke or rumblings often heard deep within the mountain. On a clear day, the 18,600-foot cone is visible from Tehran, fifty miles away.

7- 9- Talar-e Belerian, Golestan Palace, Tehran

10- 12- Takht-e Marmar (Marbel Throne), the Royal Porch, and
tile-works of Golestan Palace

The Jame' Mosque of Saveh

The Jame' Mosque built in the form of a four-iwan mosque, possesses a vast courtyard. Its original construction belongs to the Seljuq era but the present elegant complex of structures, dates from the Mongol and Safavid periods. There is a mosaic-tile inscription in the iwan, which bears the date (1520 A.D.). The mosque's artistic value, lies in a tile cupola, a mihrab decorated with beautiful plaster-mouldings, and two inscriptions in Riqa' characters. Its brick minaret which, according to its Kufic inscription, date from 504 A.H. (1100 A.D.), possesses beautiful decorations belonging to the Seljuq period.

The cupola of this mosque is covered with turquoise-colored tiles. The inner surface of the cupola is decorated with geometrical designs and tiles, and the wall of the hall under the cupola, with hexagonal turquoise colored tiles. The plaster mihrab of the mosque which has been painted in various colors, is highly attractive and beautiful.

The present Masjid-e Jom'eh of the Saveh is one of structures dating from the early Safavid era and the reign of Shah Esma'il, the first sovereign of this dynasty.

Qom

The shrines of Hazrat-e Ma'soumeh at Qom, is one of the most sacred places of Shi'ite pilgrimage in Iran. Qom's importance as a pilgrimage center dates primarily from the rule of the Safavid monarchs who, after embracing Shi'ite Islam, generously endowed its major shrines.

Qom bazaar caters to the thousands of pilgrims who visit the Shrine of Hazrat-e Ma'soumeh. Its shops offer a wide range of items such as prayer beads, candles, protective amulets, ceramic vases, essence of jasmine, and a special Qom sweet called *sowhan* which is a flat wafer made of honey and tasting like butterscotch.

13- 15- Views of Damavand and Tehran suburbs

16-17- Saveh Jame' Mosque and its elaborated mihrab (Prayer niche)

Northeastern Iran

Mashhad

Center of Shi'ite pilgrimage, capital of Khorasan Province and also for a time of the whole of Iran, Mashhad is situated in an altitude of 970 m. in the Kashaf-rud valley, a tributary of Hari-rud, between the Binalud and Hezar Masjid mountains in a rich agricultural region. For centuries, it has been an important trade center and junction point on caravan routes and highways from India to Iran and from north to south between Turkestan towns and Sea of Oman. Although much of Khorasan is mountainous, there are many fertile valleys, and the province produces large quantities of fruit, nuts, sugar beet and cotton. Mashhad is connected to Tehran by two roads (875 km., southern and 925 km. northern), railway and air. It occupies a position in the northeast of the country very similar to that of Tabriz in the northwest. Both cities, besides being relatively close to the frontiers, stand on what have often proved to be invasion routes. In consequence, Mashhad (with 1,820,631 inhabitants), like Tabriz, has frequently been attacked and sometimes captured by hostile forces. Actually, the whole province of Khorasan has been the funnel through which armies have passed from time immemorial.

Once on the ground, the traveler is fascinated by the golden cupolas and minarets. It is interesting to know that the word Mashhad - or more correctly Mashhad-e Moqaddas (the Holy Mashhad) -literally means place of martyrdom (or place of burial of a martyr).

However, the Shrine of Imam Reza and the surrounding buildings do together comprise one of the marvels of the Islamic world. Under certain constraints it is perfectly possible even for the non-Muslim to visit it; going to Iran and not doing so is a little like going to Italy and missing Vatican. The shrine itself is strictly closed to non-Muslims (save under exceptional circumstances with the special permission of the religious authorities, applied for through the Tourist Office), but it is not generally a problem to visit the rest of the complex, so long as you don't try to enter any of the buildings. You will have to dress extremely conservatively and behave yourself impeccably, and you should avoid visiting during large religious gatherings or in the main pilgrimage season (late June to mid July).

Shrine of Imam Reza

Imam Reza, heir to the Abbasid Caliphate as well as eighth of the Shi'ite Imams, died in what was then the village of Sanabad in 817 A.D. after eating some grapes. The story spread that he had been poisoned on the orders of the Caliph Ma'mun after having in some way arousing his enmity. Whatever the truth, Ma'mun buried him in a tower in Sanabad next to the tomb of his own father, the famous Harun-al Rashid, and in time this burial place began to attract Shi'ite pilgrims.

Mausoleum of Sheikh-e Jam

This mausoleum, once a part of the Khaneqah of the famous mystic Sheikh-ol Islam Ahmad Jami, dates from the (14th cent. A.D.). The present structures and their additions, however, date from the (15th to 17th cent. A.D.).

The tomb of the Sheikh-ol Islam is found within stone railings under the shade of a wild fig tree, in front of a magnificent and lofty iwan.

The Mosque with a white dome is one of the structures attached to the mausoleum built in (1235 A.D.), and later repaired (1303 A.D.) by the order of Malek Ghias-od Din Kart, and further expanded. Similarly, the adjoining Madrasah is an addition by the Timurid Shahrokh and was constructed in (1442 A.D.). In the reign of Shah Abbas I, further repairs, including tile-works, were undertaken in the year (1613 A.D.).

A magnificent souvenir, namely a stone inscription by the Mongol emperor Homayoun dated 981 A.H.(1573 A.D.) was also in this monument and has, along with four volumes of Tafsir or commentary of the Holy Koran, been removed to the Iran Bastan Museum for safe keeping.

Tomb of Loqman Baba

The Tomb of Sheikh Loqman, a well-known (10th. cent. A.D.) mystic, is one of the most remarkable of Iran's historic buildings. It consists of a brick dome, a lofty iwan, and plaster mouldings and brick decorations.

In its present state, the tomb is a low brick double-dome, separated from the polygonal body and base of the structure by a circular entablature. An embrasure is provided upon each side of the polygonal body for lighting purposes.

The foundations which support the heavy dome and the other parts covered by the dome, are beautifully constructed of strong brick in various decorative motifs. Inside the false arches, there are lozenge - shaped geometrical ornamentations, some in relief and others deep set, and all combining to produce a gracefully detailed decorative covering upon the main brick construction.

On the portal of the monument an excellent piece of plaster moulding, and inside the place, a beautiful inscription in Naskh style are to be seen, of which the latter states that the tomb was erected in (1356 A.D.) for Sheikh Mahmoud Ibn-e Mohammad. This colossal tomb bears close resemblance to that of the Seljuq Soltan Sanjar, and its interior decorations are very much similar to those of the Gonbad-e Haruniyeh in Tus. In short, this monument with its plaster mouldings and brick decorations, ranks among the most remarkable of Iran's historical and artistic remains.

19-21- Views of Mashhad and its souvenirs

22- 23- Sheikh Ahmad Jami (Mystic sufi) Mausoleum, Torbat-e Jam

24- A man from Khwaf, Khorasan

Karat Minaret

This is a historic brick tower upon a hillock outside the village of Karat, Tabas, to the south of Khorasan province. In addition, the village has been provided with a fortified wall and rampart. According to a Kuffic inscription, the minaret is a historic relic from the 11th century A.D.

Khwaf Windmills

Windmill was a contraption of the Khwaf villagers from times immemorial in their endless struggle to harness the desert wind energy and grind wheat into flour. The village was a flourishing fruit and silk production center by the 9th century A.D. Now its products include wheat, pomegranate, and grape. The terraced clay walls in the middle of the village support several windmills elevated on a raised platform.

Monastery of Bayazid-e Bastami , Bastam

A conical domed brick structure, with a lofty iwan, and a stone minaret, Bayazid's Mausoleum and the resting-place of Amir Afghani, date from the 14th and 19th centuries A.D. Most of the structures belong to the reign of Oljaitu, the Muslim Il-khan of Mongol period. There is a plaster inscription in Thulth calligraphy, on top of the mihrab and beside Bayazid's tomb and several others, and a Char Taqi (four-arched square structure) adjoining the mausoleum, where Amir Afghani is buried, and which is dated 1869 A.D. Upon Amir Afghani's tombstone several lines of verse have been inscribed in Nasta'liq style and the names of the calligrapher and the sculptor are given at the end as Mohammad Rahim Harati and Seyyed Hasan Mashhadi, respectively. The Jame'' Mosque stands on the southeastern side of the mausoleum, next to a high, fluted tower called Kashaneh. The whole complex belongs to the 14th century A.D.

The Minaret of Masjid-e Jame', Damghan

Located in Damghan, this 31-meter high minaret, to the north of the Jame' Mosque, dates from the Seljuq period. Altogether consisting of 105 steps, it is made of brick and possesses tile decorations from the twelfth century A.D., in its upper part. Its surface has been decorated with a Chapter of the Holy Koran. The Jame' Mosque has been constructed at a later date. If, as suggested by some experts, the tile-work of the minaret be of the same date as the minaret itself, then these tile decorations will probably be older than those of the village Sin, in Isfahan (1131 A.D.).

28- Cheshmeh Ali, Damghan ▶
29- 32- Next Page, a 19th century pavilion, Bayazid-e Bastami Mausoleum, Bastam, Old gate, Semnan, Minaret of Jame' Mosque, Damghan.

27- Khwaf wind-mill, northern Khorasan

Northern Iran

Gilan and Mazandaran

This includes the whole area to the south of the Caspian Sea, saltwater lake in southeastern Europe and southwestern Asia, the largest inland body of water in the world. It is bordered on the south by Iran, conforming to three provinces of Gilan, Mazandaran, and Golestan, from west to east. The southern and southwestern shorelines of the Caspian Sea are bordered by the Alborz Mountains and the Caucasus Mountains. The sea has numerous tributaries, notable the Volga, Ural, and Zhem rivers, all of which flow into it from the north. Other tributaries include the Gorgan and Atrak rivers, flowing from the east, and the Kura River, flowing from the west. The sea has no outlet. The Caspian Sea is linked to the Baltic Sea, the White Sea, and the Black Sea by an extensive network of inland waterways, chief of which is the Volga River. These waterways provide an outlet to northern Europe for the oil fields of Baku, Azerbaijan on the Absheron Peninsula. The Caspian Sea also contains highly productive fisheries, yielding valuable catches of sturgeon (the chief source of caviar), salmon. Perch, herring, and carp. Other animal life in the Caspian Sea includes tortoises, porpoises, and seals.

Navigation is frequently dangerous because of violent southeastern storms, and during the winter months the northern parts of the Caspian Sea are closed by ice. The chief ports along the Iranian shores are Astara, Anzali, Nowshahr, and Bandar-e Turkman.

Masuleh

There are many traditional and unspoiled mountain villages throughout Gilan and Mazandaran, but one of the most breathtaking beautiful ones is Masuleh , 56 km south –west of Rasht and 1050 metres above seal level. Approached from Fuman by a dramatic mountain pass and completely surrounded by forest, this perfectly preserved village appears to have grown put of its surroundings like a limpet clinging to a rock. It's formed of several irregular levels of terraced, pale cream houses with gray slate roofs, interspersed with evergreen trees, so steep is the slope that the familiar Iranian network of narrow alleys is entirely absent, and instead of the flat roof of each level of houses forms a pathway for the level above.

34- Beach of Babolsar, Caspian Sea, Mazandaran

35-Darreh (valley) Dohezar, Tonekabon

36-37- Forest dwellers, northern Iran

◀ Masuleh village, Gilan

39-Village of Kelardasht, Mazandaran

41- A Turkman tent, Golestan Province

Gorgan

Gorgan is a city in northeastern Iran, located near the Caspian Sea, and the capital of Golestan province. Gorgan lies about 37 km. (about 23 mi.) inland from the port of Bandar-e Turkman. Gorgan is the center of an intensively cultivated farming region whose major commercial crops are wheat, cotton, and fruits. Before the 1930s the city was known as Astarabad. It has existed since at least the Achaemenian empire (550?-330? B. C.), and excavations at nearby Turang

42- A Turkman woman weaving traditional rug

Teppeh recovered various bronze objects dating to 500 B.C. by the 1st century A.D. Astarabad had become a well-established stop on the famous Silk Road from China to the Mediterranean Sea. Until the 1200 s, the city flourished as a commercial and intellectual center. From the 13th to the early 20th centuries, the city suffered frequent raids by rival armies and renegade Turkish tribesmen, and the resulting insecurity contributed to the economic decline of Astarabad.

Northwestern Iran

Tabriz, Ardebil and Zanjan

Lying at an altitude of 1,400 meters above sea level, 619 km. northwest of Tehran, provincial capital of East Azerbaijan, the second largest city in Iran until the late 1960's and one of its former capitals (with a population of 1,305,000 according to 1996 census), Tabriz is located in the 160 km. long Aji Chai or Talkheh-rud valley to the north of the long ridge of Mount Sahand. The valley opens out into a plain that slopes down gently to the northern end of Lake Urumiyeh, 60 km. to the west. It can be reached by good road, rail (742 km. from Tehran, with connections to Europe and Moscow), and air from Tehran and other major cities.

By virtue of its situation, Tabriz has an agreeable summer climate, but the cold in winter is severe. Altogether, it has a continental climate with low humidity. The average annual rainfall is 288 mm. Its worst natural disadvantage, however, is its vulnerability to earthquakes, one of which utterly destroyed the city in 858 A.D. Rebuilt in a minor key, it was again devastated in 1041 A.D., when more than 40,000 people lost their lives.

The town has a long and checkered history: although the early history of Tabriz is shrouded in legend and mystery, its origins are believed to date back to distant antiquity, perhaps even before the Sassanian era (224-651 A.D.). The oldest stone tablet with a reference to Tabriz is that of Sargon II, the Assyrian King. The tablet refers to a place called Tauris Castle and Tarmkis. The historians believe that this castle was situated on the site of the present Tabriz. It was the capital of Azerbaijan in the 3rd century A.D. and again under the Mongol Il-khanid dynasty (1256-1353), although for some time Maragheh supplanted it.

During the reign of Aqa Khan of the Il-khanids, as well as under the reign of Ghazan Khan, Tabriz reached the peak of glory and importance. Many great artists and philosophers from all over the world traveled to Tabriz. During this same period Khwajeh Rashid-od Din Fazlollah, the learned historian and Minister of Ghazan Khan, built the famous Rab'-e Rashidi center.

In 1392, after the end of Mongol rule, the town was sacked by Tamerlane. It was soon restored under the Turkmen tribe of the Qara Qoyounlu, who established a short-lived local dynasty. Under the Safavids it rose from regional to national capital for a short period, but the second of the Safavid kings, Shah Tahmasp, moved the capital to Qazvin because of the vulnerability of Tabriz to Ottoman attacks. The town then went into a period of decline, fought over by the Iranians, Ottomans and Russians (the later occupying it several times in the first half of 20th century, including most of both World Wars), and struck by earthquake and disease. The Iranian Constitutional Revolution originated in Tabriz and culminated during the reign of

Mohammad Ali Shah of Qajar dynasty (1779-1925). Sattar Khan and Baqer Khan were the two most prominent leading figures behind the movement.

Most places of tourist interest are to the south of the river crossing the town and along or north of Imam Khomeini Avenue: Azerbaijan Museum, constructed in 1957 and inaugurated in 1962, is on Imam Khomeini Ave. (next to the Blue Mosque). No one can miss the very large and 15th-century covered bazaar of Tabriz, with its architectural style, numerous caravanserais, mosques, and schools that add further beauty and glory to this complex. The Blue Mosque (or Masjid-e Kabud) on the north side of Imam Khomeini Ave., is a 15th-century structure destroyed by one of Tabriz's recurrent earthquakes. Despite showing a sorry ruin, it was recently restored with the utmost skill. Because of the blue tiles used in the decoration of both interior and exterior of the mosque, it has become to be known as the *Turquoise of Islam*. Citadel of Tabriz (also called Masjid-e Alishah and Arge-e Tabriz) in Imam Khomeini Ave. is the impressive remainder of a great and imposing building in the town. Il Goli or the National Park (former Shah Goli), is a pleasant hillside garden and park around an artificial lake to the area of 54,675 square meters in the style of the much smaller Bagh-e Takht north of Shiraz or the Qasr-e Qajar north of Tehran. Known as the Sho'ara Cemetery, the Mausoleum is the resting place of more than fifty famous Iranian poets, mystics, scientists, and theologians in Seqat-ol Eslam Avenue. During the years which led to the Constitutional Revolution and afterwards, Constitutional House (next to the Tabriz grand bazaar, on Motahhari Ave.) was used as the gathering place of the leaders, activists, and the sympathizers of the movement. As the legend goes, the first people to settle here were the soldiers involved in military operations nearly 800 years ago, who found the cones by chance and used them as their temporary camouflage and accommodation. However, among archaeologists, it is considered to be of Pre-Islamic Period.

Tomb of Sheikh Safi, Ardebil

Sheikh Safi-od Din Eshaq was a Sufi saint who died at Ardebil in 1334, and is regarded as the founder of the Safavid Dynasty. "Allah dome" was built over the body of Sheikh Safi soon after his death, on the site where the saint lived and met with his disciples during his lifetime. Its glazed-brick decoration repeats the name of God, and the circular plaque below the inscriptional frieze records the name of the tomb's architect, Awad Ibn-e Mohammad. The shrine prospered through the patronage of the Safavid kings, and it is recorded that a thousand people a day were fed from the shrine's kitchens. In 1611 Shah Abbas I donated his porcelain collection to the shrine which was kept in hundreds of wall niches inside a large domed building called the Chini Khaneh or China Room. The lands and possessions of the shrine were dispersed in the eighteenth century and with them the vitality of a fascinating religious and social institution.

44-45- Il Goli park and pavilion, municipality of Tabriz, 19th century

46- Mirza Shafi'e Timcheh (Carpet Seller) Tabriz

47- Tabriz carpet

48- 49- Sheikh Safi Mausoleum, Ardebil

50-54- Saint Stephanous Cathedral, Jolfa, West Azerbaijan

The church of St. Stepanus, located 16 kilometers to the south-east of Julfa, dates back to the 8th century A.H. (14th cent. A.D.) and later, and is remarkable for its pyramidal roof cover and facade decorations.

The monument is also known under the name of the church of Darreh Sham.

55-56- Oljaitu Tomb, Soltaniyeh, Zanjan

Soltaniyeh - the town of Soltans- 285 km. to the northwest of Tehran in Zanjan Province. Mausoleum of Soltaniyeh was built by the Mongols as belated expiation for the wholesale destruction they wrought during the conquest of Iran. Arghun Khan founded Soltaniyeh in the last decade of the 13th century, and it was enhanced during the reign of his sons Ghazan and Oljaitu during the early 14th century.

It is difficult to recall a mausoleum equaling the grandeur of this one anywhere else in Iran. Visible from far across the surrounding plain, the mausoleum's very striking egg-shaped dome is said to be the largest Islamic version ever built.

The mausoleum is 53 meters high and 25 meters in diameter. Octagonal in shape, it is dominated by a superb dome that soars almost as impressively without the eight elegant minarets or superb portals that no longer survive.

Western Iran

Kermanshah

The capital of Kermanshah Province, in an altitude of 1,630 m. above sea level, Kermanshah is 525 km. to the southwest of Tehran. Being a populous city of 631,199 inhabitants, mainly Kords, it stands, like Hamadan, on the great highway that connected Baghdad and the West with Iranian Plateau. First built on a site a few km. from the present town, it probably dates from the 4th century A.D. Its vulnerable position has always rendered it liable to incursions, and it was in turn captured by the Arabs in 649 A.D., the Buyids in the 10th century A.D., soon after by the Seljuqs, and then sacked by Mongols in the early 13th century. After several centuries of relative peace and prosperity, its strategic position on the road to Baghdad brought trouble in the form of very heavy Iraqi missile and bomb attacks during the Iraqi war against Iran (1980-88). The town's situation is highly picturesque, and it is one of the liveliest market-centers of the province.

Kermanshah Museum is located in Dr Shari'ati Avenue, Shahid Haddad-e Adel Street, in a famous building called Tekiyeh Mo'aven-ol Molk (locally known as Hosainiyeh), which is one of the historical monuments from the Qajar period.

Buildings and places of interest around Kermanshah are as follows: the rock carvings and inscriptions of Darius I at Bisotun, 32 km. east of Kermanshah, in addition to which you will see the relief of a bearded reveler (probably Hercules) with a goblet of wine recently discovered near the main road; the relief and inscriptions at Taq-e Bostan; the two staircases of the temple of Anahita at Kangavar; the Taq-e Gara (believed to be Sassanian, but the actual date is the subject of much controversy) near the top of the Pay-e Taq pass, approximately 90 km. west of the town; the ruins of Dinavar (dating from the Selucid era to the late 14th century A.D.), 45 km. east-northeast of the town; the Mound of Kambadene (from Achaemenian to Sassanian times), just to northeast of Kermanshah; and Dokkan-e Davoud , a Median tomb of 7th century B.C., 3 km. from Sar-e Pol-e Zahab, which shows a praying man on a rock piece.

Achaemenian Bas-relief at Bisotun

These historic Bas-reliefs, carved on a rock some hundred feet high adjoining the Hamadan-Kermanshah highway, belong to the Achaemenian period. These sculptures of considerable dimensions comprise the figure of Darius, tall with attractive features, and Ahura Mazda's symbolic celestial figure above his head. Darius has stretched his right hand toward this deity

57-60- Taq-e Gara (watchman site), Sassanian era (4th century A.D.), a Kordish woman, Nan-e Berenji

(traditional sweet), and a Median tomb (7th century B.C.), all in Kermanshah

and with his left foot tramples upon the rebel Gaumata lying prostrate at his feet. Two persons are standing behind Darius, while nine prisoners of war from different nations are seen before him with their hands tied behind their backs and a cord running around their necks.

The Bisotun (Behistun) inscriptions are in three languages, Babylonian, Elamite and Old Persian, and are known as the Longer and the Shorter inscriptions. The former consists of Ahura Mazda's praise and adoration, the genealogy of Darius, and an account of the events of his reign, his views, beliefs, recommendations, and commands. The other and shorter inscription deals with Darius's lineage and some of the events of his reign.

These sculptures seem to have been intended to give a true picture of those represented. The Achaemenian sovereign, for instance, is carved with long beard and hair, wearing a garment with folds at the waist. His height is 180 centimeters. One of the two persons standing behind the king, bears the royal bow and arrows, while the other is holding the king's spear. The figure of Ahura Mazda is seen above the heads of the prisoners, with a winged sun-disc encircling him, the symbol of eternity. In the inscriptions, Darius gives the names of his ancestors and says:

"Eight of my family were kings before me. I am the ninth. We inherit kingship on both sides." The Bisotun sculptures are of the highest historic importance and were created in 480 B.C., the sixth year of Darius's reign.

Sassanian Bas-relief at Taq-e Bostan

The Sassanian remains in Taq-e Bostan comprise two arches one smaller than the other, both entrances to grottoes, and a sculptured space on the outside. The grottoes have been cut into the mountain rock on the face of which the sculpture has been executed. The exterior carvings of the greater arch include the figure of two winged angels holding a ring, while inside the grotto, the figure of Khosrow II can be seen with other reliefs covering the interior of the arcade, consisting of the king's hunting scenes, and figures of boatsmen and musicians. (590-627 A.D.). In the smaller arch next to the first one, there are two bas-reliefs representing Shapur II and Shapur III, with two inscriptions in Pahlavi script and language. The sculpture on the exterior of the arch shows three people, and the whole scene is said to represent the coronation of Ardeshir II. In this sculpture, the figure of Ardeshir Babakan and that of Mithra, the sun god, have also remained in good condition. (212-226 A.D.)

From under the Taq-e Bostan rock a stream flows out and the historic bas-reliefs overlook a pleasant park with a large pool and beautiful lawns. A rampart and parapet wall constructed above the grotto are representative of the architectural and sculptural techniques of the Sassanian period, as are the arches and their ornamentations. Above the figure of Khosrow II inside the grotto, there is an expanse of stone supported by columns cut into the rock and representing three sculptured figures, of which the one in the middle is the figure of a king who has put the point of his sword on the ground, with his right hand stretched out to receive a wreath from another person standing on his left, while on his right there is a woman pouring water from a vase. Some archaeologists believe this figure to be the image of Anahita, the Goddess of rivers and streams.

The greatest of the Taq-e Bostan sculptures is undoubtedly that of Khosrow II, the Sassanian monarch, mounted on a huge horse, and clad in an armour and holding a spear in his right hand and a round buckler, in the left, while his quiver can be seen further to the left. This great relief sculpture executed upon a mountain rock is one of the finest of its kind.

61-Houbeh Strait (Rijab)

◄ 62- Victory of Darius over rebels, 4th century B.C., Bisotun

63- Sassanian Carving, 7th Century, Taq-e Bostan

A study of these sculptures will also supply some very interesting information on various types of arms used in that period and details of garments worn by courtiers, soldiers and ordinary people, which will be of tremendous value to those interested in the history of military techniques and court ceremonies under the Sassanian rulers.

The Taq- e Bostan sculptures represent the pomp and majesty of the Sassanian court, particularly during the reign of Khosrow II (590-627 A.D.), and various scenes, such as coronation ceremonies the adoration of Ahura Mazda, and show of respect to the Mobads, or Zoroastrian religious leaders.

64-66- Investiture of a Sassanian king by Anahita and Ahura Mazda,
King Khosrow I (Sassaniam king), mounted on Shabdiz (his famous horse),
Taq-e Bostan

67-71-Tile-works of Mo'aven-ol Molk Tekiyeh, 19th century, Kermanshah

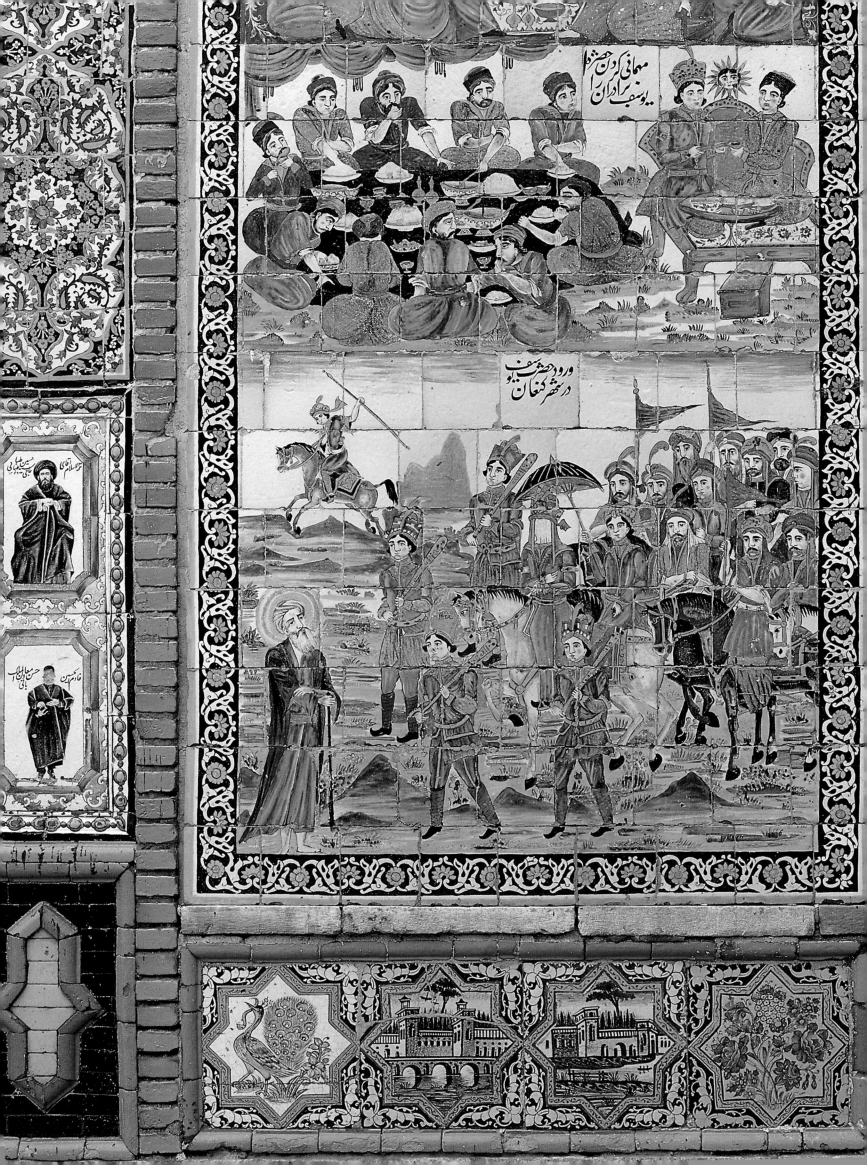

مهمانی کردن در حضرت
یوسف برادران را

ورود حضرت یوسف
در شهر کنعان

تولای اسلام آقای
حسین علی تقی

خادم حسین
حسن معین الملک بانی

◄72- Rijab River, Kermanshah

73- A Kord man

74-75- Baba Yadegar (mystic sufi) Mausoleum, Rijab, Kermanshah

Hamadan

A city in western Iran, located in a productive farming region. The capital of Hamadan Province, the city is known for the manufacture of rugs, leather trunks, ceramics, and copper ware. It is the center of the Iranian shellac and leather trade and is commercially important because of its position on the principal route between Baghdad and Tehran. The city of Hamadan has a number of bazaars and several mosques. Also in the city are two tombs of special interest, one claimed to be that of the Biblical Mordecai and Esther, and the other that of the Islamic philosopher-physician Avicenna. The city is believed to occupy the site of the city of Ecbatana, capital of the ancient Medes. During World War I (1914-1918), Hamadan was the scene of fighting between Russian and Turk-German forces. The city was held at various times by the Russians, the Turks, and the British before being restored to Iranian government control in 1918. The town's places of interest are: Avicenna's tomb and Museum, tomb of Baba Taher (Iranian mystic and wandering dervish who died in 1019 A.D., and Ganjnameh, Hamadan's oldest Achaemenian rock carvings consisting of two huge inscribed panels (twenty lines) carved on two rock faces of some two meters in height, located 5 km. west of the city on the slopes of Mount Alvand.

The Ganjnameh (or Jangnami) Achaemenian inscriptions

The Achaemenian Ganjnameh (Treasure Inventory) is a lengthy inscription in cuneiform script, composed in three parts (in Old Persian, Elamite and Babylonian) and carved on the face of two rocks of some two meters in height, on the mountain Alvand. These twenty-line inscriptions, belonging to Darius I and Xerxes, consist of a genealogical account of the Achaemenian monarchs and the adoration of Ahura Mazda. Here is the translation of the text concerning Xerxes:

"The Great God Ahura Mazda, greatest of all the gods, who created this earth and the sky and the people who gave happiness to the people who made Xerxes king an outstanding king among many kings, an outstanding ruler among innumerable rulers; I (am) the great king Xerxes, king of kings, king of lands with numerous inhabitants, king of this vast kingdom with far-away territories, son of the Achaemenian monarch Darius."

The Parthian Stone Lion

This stone statue of a lion has been attributed by some scholars to the Median period, by others to the Achaemenian era, and still by another group, to the times of the Parthian rulers. The statue is about 2½ meters in length and 1½ meters in width, and it now rests upon a stone base provided for it in 1949 A.D.

77- Darius and Xerxes inscriptions, (4th century B.C.), Hamadan

78-Achaemenian stone lion , (4th century B.C.), Hamadan

◀ 79- Bu Ali (Avicenna) Tomb (scientist), 980 A.D.,

80- Baba Taher (poet) Tomb, 1910, Hamadan

81- Bazaar, Hamadan

82- Poshti (Pillow) sellers, Khorramabad , Lorestan

Khorramabad

A city in western Iran, located in the Zagros Mountains, and capital of the province of Lorestan. Khorramabad is a market center for the farm products of the region and an industrial center manufacturing synthetic fibers and processed foods. The famous Lorestan bronzes (4000? B. C.) were recovered in the early 20th century from a nearby site. Because the city is situated strategically in a river gap of the Zagros Mountains, it has been used for passage between the lowland plain of Khuzestan and the highland central plateau, and thus has been the site of many battles over the centuries. The city is home to the Black Fortress (Falak-ol Aflak Fortress), the ruins of a fort-palace complex built between the mid-12th and 15th centuries and used as the official residence of Lorestan's governors for more than 400 years. Brick Minaret is a 30-m. high cylindrical brick structure of the Islamic period of city's history. Gerdab-e Sangi is another historic monument of (probably) Sassanian period in the city. In Boroujerd to the north of Lorestan Province, one can visit Jame' Mosque which is a relic of Qajar period (1874-75 A. D.).

83- 85- Nature of Lorestan, Bisheh Waterfall and Gahar Lake, Lorestan, Western Iran.

86- Khorramabad, general view of the city

87-90-Views of Khorramabad (top), brick minaret, Falak-ol Aflak

Citadel (down), cistern (6ᵗʰ A.D.), early Islamic inscription

91- Boroujerd Jame' Mosque

Central Iran

Isfahan

Isfahan, with a population of 1,159,102 (1992 census), is and has been the capital of the province of Isfahan since 900 years. The elevation of the city is 1,570 meters above sea level. Giving purity to the air under the brilliant blue sky and often violet-hued mountains. It is connected to Tehran by air (regular daily flights), rail and road.

The most famous Persian description of the city of Isfahan is *Isfahan nesf-e Jahan* (Isfahan is half the world), which the Isfahanis coined in the 16th century to express the city's grandeur. Isfahan, chosen and designed capital under Shah Abbas I, was reconstituted with so many new mosques, palaces, bridges, avenues and parks that even European travelers wrote rapturously of its beauties. Knight Jean Chardin, a dependable observer according to A. U. Pope, reports that in 1666 Isfahan had 162 mosques, 48 *madrasahs* (schools), 182 caravanserais and 173 baths.

Isfahan steelworks started production in 1971 and is planned to double its present output of 1,900,000 tons in the coming years and make Iran self-sufficient as regards steel production. The Zayandeh-rud river watering gardens and fields with its numerous tributaries along its 360-km. course, flows from west to east through the city, and divides off Jolfa and some other suburbs from the main part of the city, but most of the main attractions are to the north of the river.

Chehel Sotun Palace

Built as a reception hall by Shah Abbas I (1657 A.D.) behind the Ali Qapu Palace continues the old *talar*, or columnar porch. At its simplest it is only a roof-high porch constituting the façade. When attached to a royal building, it provides a huge outdoor reception hall, and is susceptible to lavish embellishments, which have included mirror-plated columns, panels and stalactites, and polychrome mosaic ceilings.

The name means "The Forty Columns", although there are actually 20. A reflecting pool is provided to see the other 20. A more mundane explanation is that 40 was once used synonymously with *many* in Persian, and still is in some quarters. Walls of Chehel Sotun were covered with frescoes and paintings depicting specific historical scenes.

Imam Mosque

Imam Mosque, also called Masjid-e Shah (Royal Mosque) before the victory of Islamic Revolution, begun in 1612, and, despite Shah Abbas' impatience, under construction until 1638, represents the culmination of a thousand years of mosque building in Iran. The half-domed arch of outer portal on the square, understood as an aspect of the square rather than of the mosque, is the most thrilling example of human artifice that could be imagined. Its height amounts to 30 m., the flanking minarets are 40 m. tall - with the sanctuary minarets higher still - and the sanctuary double-shell dome soaring not less than 54 m.

Ali Qapu Palace

The first skyscraper of Iran with a marvelous view over the public Maidan and city to the front and the Shah's pleasure gardens at the back, it is seven floors tall, accessible by a difficult staircase, square in plan, probably a northern type, with the *talar* as the second story. All the little rooms have points of interest. A huge reception hall capable of holding two hundred or more courtiers, its interior was covered with delicate polychrome relief.

On the sixth floor, niches shaped like bowls or high-stemmed flasks are dug into the wall. Their purpose is not only decorative but also acoustical, since here was a music room. Many of the beautiful murals and mosaics which once decorated the many small rooms, corridors and stairways have been destroyed, partly in the Qajar period and as a result of natural causes in recent years.

Talar-e Ashraf (Ashraf Hall), Isfahan

In its present state, the Talar-e Ashraf consists of a large hall and two adjoining chambers. The building belongs to the reigns of the Safavid monarchs Shah Abbas II and Shah Solaiman, (1642-1694 A.D.).

The present complex of structures known as the Talar-e Ashraf consists of the remaining parts of the Safavid palace and its golden decorations, artistic ornaments frescoes and proportionate arcades are particularly attractive and highly valuable.

Madrasah Chahar Bagh

The construction of this madrasah marked the end of a sustained and brilliant period in the history of architecture. After the death of Shah Abbas I in 1627 the dynasty's decline began, although architectural styles, developed so gradually, were a little slower in dissipating. The madrasah was built on the initiative of Shah Soltan Hosain's mother between 1706 and 1714, and was the scene of the execution of this unhappy monarch and the extinction of the Safavid dynasty at the hands of Afghan invaders in 1722.

93- Chehel Sotun Palace

Friday Mosque

Also called Masjid-e Jom'eh, a brisk half-hour from the square, is the most ancient and in some ways the most interesting building in the city, and hence in Iran. It was built late in the 11th and early 12th century as a focus for the town. Changes and additions were made in subsequent periods. Therefore, it is a landmark in the evolution of Iranian sacred architecture.

It is not as immediately attractive to the external eye as the complex of Maidan-e Imam except for the tile-work of fifteenth century in the great courtyard and mihrab of Oljaitu, but the complex harmony of its components makes of it a palimpsest both meaningful in its details and aesthetically pleasing in their superimposition. Every architectural age of Iran (except the most decadent) can be observed and studies in this mosque. The western *iwan* is usually the first element to attract the visitor's attention. The architecture of the apse is also different from that of the Safavid mosques: there are no pendentives or complicated stalactites to overload the vault that is made up of large alveoli of very pure design.

Vank Cathedral

This is a world-famous architectural monument of the Safavid period in New Jolfa. The belfry faces the main entrance. There is a small museum (originally built in 1930, and moved to the present-day premises in 1971) where you might be able to find a guidebook on New Jolfa in English, or someone who speaks English, as most educated Armenians do. There are as many as 13 other churches in New Jolfa as well. The next two famous ones are the Holy Mother of God and the Bethlehem. Vank Cathedral's Press was founded in 1636 and was one of the first ones in the Middle East to print the *Book of Psalms* in 1638. During its 350 years of operation the Cathedral's Press has printed about 500 books and thousands of pamphlets, etc.

Hasht Behesht Palace

This mid-17th century Safavid palace was originally surrounded by a vast garden and hundreds of similar buildings, also named *Hasht Behesht* (eight paradise) of which nothing remains except this interesting and beautiful palace. The existing two-story palace owes its fame, apart from its architectural and decorative merits, to the lavish use of marble slabs, stalactite vault decorations, excellent tile-works dotted with scenes of animals (birds, beasts of prey, and reptiles) covering the building on the outside. Structurally, it consists of a *Shah Neshin* (Royal Parlor), a verandah, numerous rooms, and *iwans* richly decorated with gilded frescoes.

Khwaju Bridge

The 132-m. long Khwaju Bridge, some 1.5 km. downstream (east) of See-o Se Pol, is slightly smaller but even more attractive, with two levels of terraces overlooking the river. Built by the order of Shah Abbas II in 1650 A.D., it has been constructed with two purposes in mind: to be used both as a roadway and a dam (by means of sluices, the level of the river may be raised or lowered at will). The original purpose of this dam was to form an artificial lake for some distance upstream, in front of the numerous palace buildings and kiosks that stood on either side of the river. It is now used to raise the level of the river sufficiently to fill irrigation canals on either side. But its most fascinating features are the pavilions set into the 12-meter width called *Shah Neshin* (Royal Parlors) and once decorated with faience and inscriptions.

See-o-Se Pol, (Allahverdi Khan Bridge)

This bridge, built on the Zayandeh-rud at the southern extremity of Chahar Bagh avenue has 33 spans and its construction, started in (1602 A.D.) by order of Shah Abbas I, was completed by Allahverdi Khan, one of the Shah's generals who had been appointed for the purpose, hence its second appellation. The bridge is 300 meters long and 14 meters wide.

Sheikh Lotfollah Mosque

This small mosque on the eastern side of the square, is datable to the first years of the seventeenth century, and was built by Shah Abbas in honor of the great Lebanese Sheikh, who was a sort of Islamic Billy Graham of his time. The enormous dome is supported by walls 170 cm. thick, and its solidity is transmuted into lightness - one would even say fragility - by two features of the utmost tact and daring: a huge aperture and several high windows to trap the maximum amount of natural light, and steadily-decreasing concentric ellipses of midnight blue with delicate white arabesques vanishing to all or nothing in the center of the dome.

The mihrab is decorated with mosaic tiles and stalactites, all of the highest artistic value, and the name of the architect, Mohammad Reza, is given in two tablets installed inside it. This is pure architecture, flawless and serene, and still as perfect as on the day of dedication more than three hundred years ago. No one in a receptive or contemplative mood can enter without a shock of the sense of being received into a Presence, for all its elegance, and finish it has no weakness: the scale is too ample, the patterns too strong.

98- Sheikh Lotfollah Mosque

99- Imam Mosque

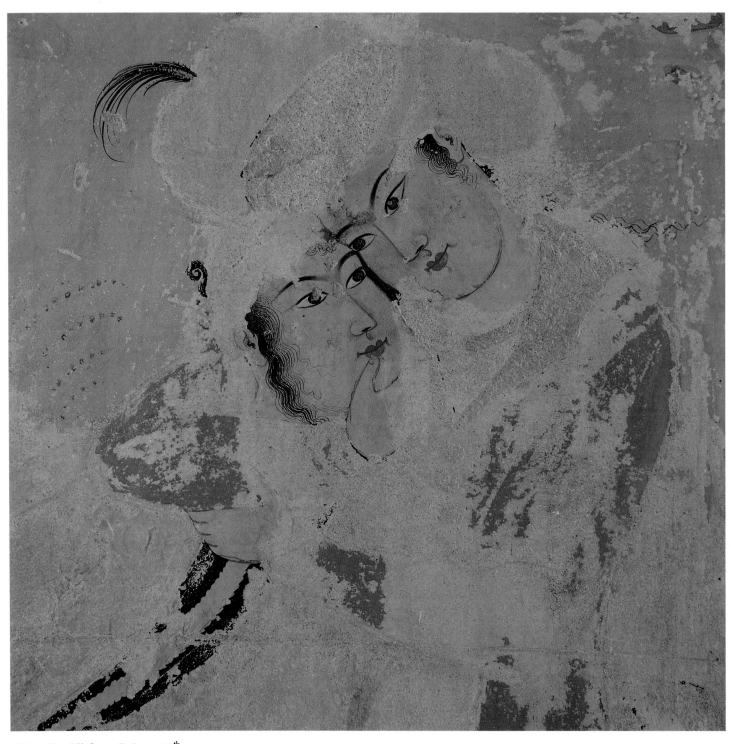

100- 103- Ali Qapu Palace, 17th century

102- Ali Qapu Palace, 17ᵗʰ century, Isfahan

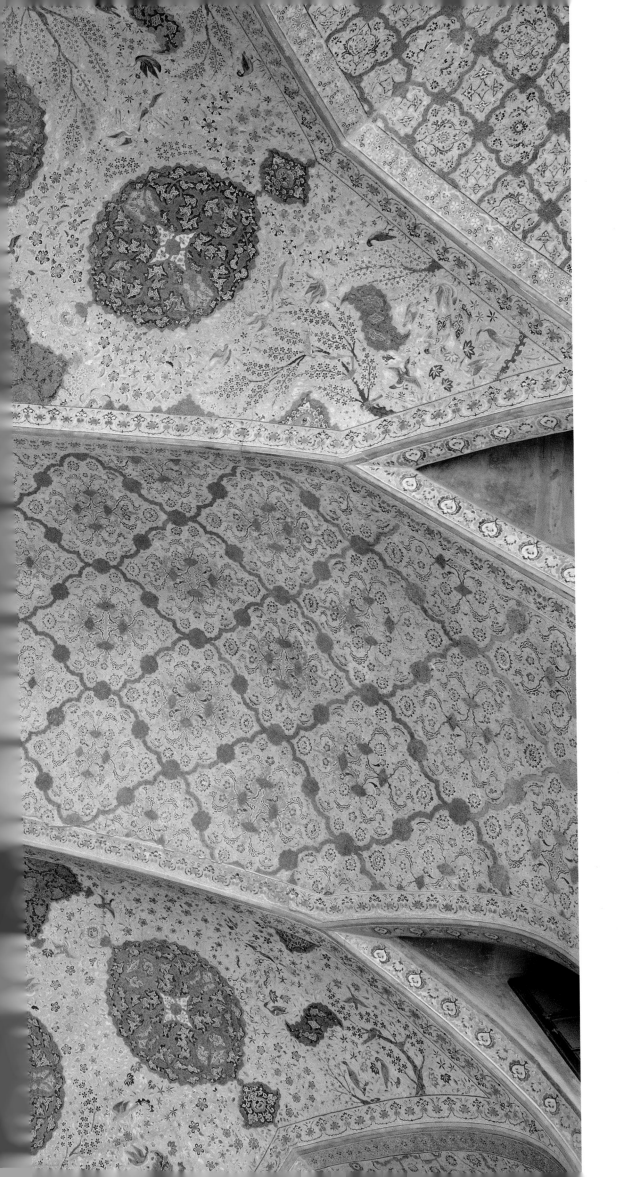

123

104- Talar-e Ashraf (Royal Hall), 17th century

105- Muqarnas vault, Chahar Bagh Madrasah, 17th century

106- Portal vault, Chahar Bagh Madrasah, 17th century

107- Bethlehem Church, 17th century

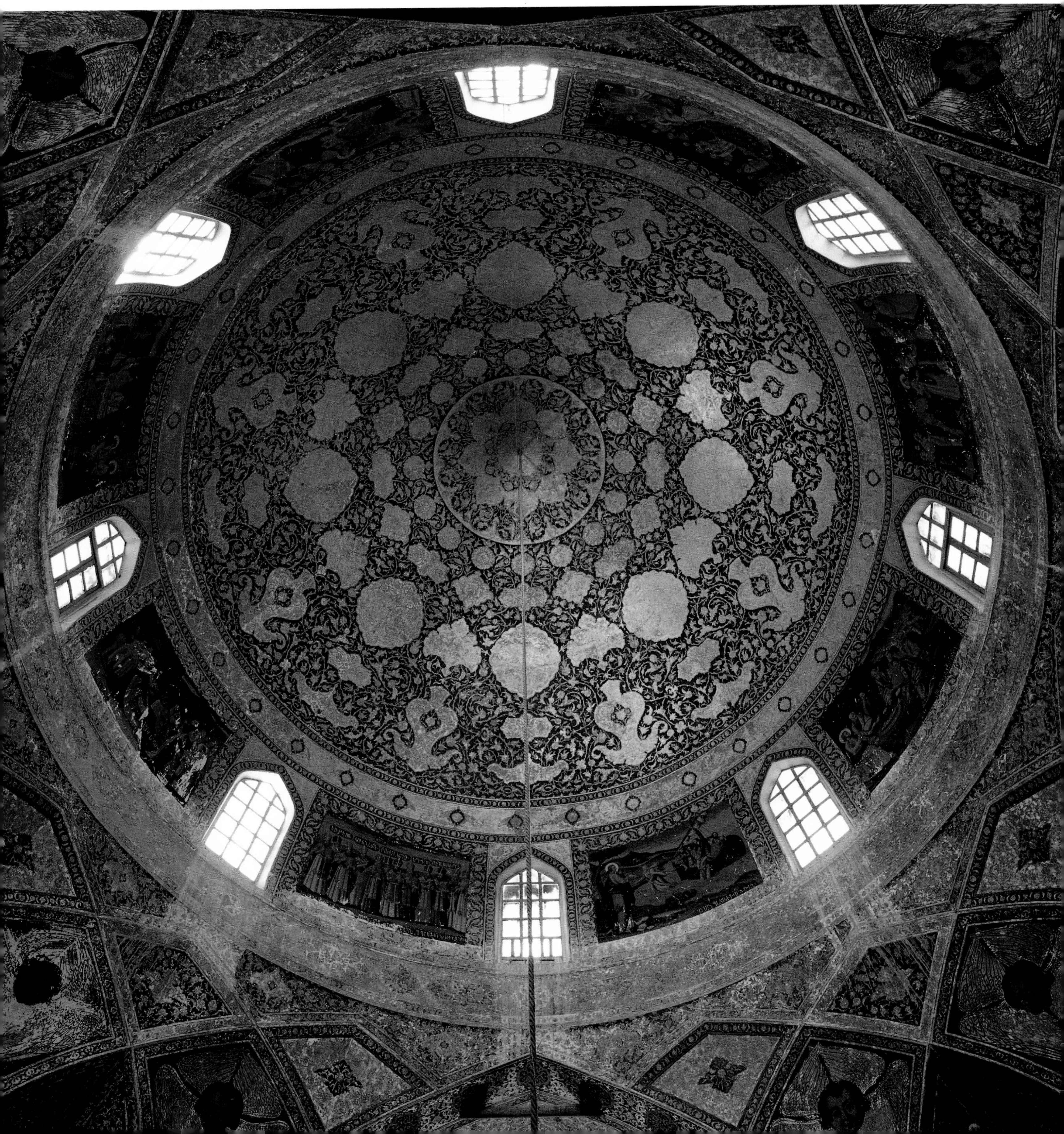

108- Vank Church

109- Interior designs of Vank Church, 17th century

111- Hasht Behesht (Eight Paradise) Palace, 17th century

112- Mirror works of Rakib Khaneh, a 19th century royal residence

113-116- Isfahani craftsmen, painting on plates (*Minakari*), and engraved souvenirs

117-120- Stamped *qalamkar* fabrics, young carpet
designer, Persian painting on ivory

121-122- Isfahan bazaar

123- Khwaju Bridge, 17th century

124-See-o Se Pol (Allahverdi Khan Bridge), 17th century

Kashan

Located in an altitude of 1,600 m. above sea level, Kashan is one of the main cities of Isfahan Province and a beautiful large oasis town on the Qom-Kerman road running along the western edge of the Great Desert, *Kevir*. It is 240 km. to the south of Tehran and 220 km. to the north of Isfahan, and can be reached via a first-class highway, national road, or railway from Tehran and Isfahan. The town's population amounts to 400,000, living on an area of 2,100 hectares.

In addition to its world-famous carpets, Kashan is also well known for its silk and the glazed earthenware tile called *kashi* after its place of manufacture. It has long been noted for its silk textiles, ceramics, copper ware, and rose water (*golab*) from the well-known rose fields of Qamsar, as well.

One of the most important archaeological sites in central Iran, it has a historical background of over 7,000 years. Majority of historians and travelers to the town have called it a gate to the world civilization. Kashan flourished mainly during the Seljuq and Safavid periods of the post-Islamic history of Iran. Samples of art works created by Kashani artisans can be seen in the famous museums of the world.

The town has many picturesque *bad-girs* (wind-towers), essential in the town's hot and airless summers before the introduction of air-conditioning. Modern industry plays a part in Kashan, in parallel with the ongoing social development. In bazaar, however, carpet-weaving, embroidery work, the making of rose water, scent, pottery, and other crafts are carried on, in much the same and with the same skill as of old.

Fin Historic Gardens

Also known as the Bagh-e Tarikhi-e Fin or Bagh-e Amir Kabir at Fin 6 km. To the southwest, it serves as the finest surviving example (since 1.000 years) in Iran, and creates the contrast between the *Kevir* region and the greenery of the well-tended oasis below the adjoining Karkas mountain. A major part of Kashan's water was supplied by the perennial source of Solaimaniyeh spring in the garden. Designed for Shah Abbas I, this classical Persian vision of paradise contains the remains of his two-story palace set around a pool. The garden has other Safavid royal buildings, although they were substantially rebuilt, and others were addend in the Qajar period. The building housing Kashan Museum was built in 1968.

Fin was the scene of a tragedy in 1852, when Mirza Taqi Khan known as Amir Kabir, the Grand Vizier of Naser-od Din Shah, was murdered there. He is considered a national hero and vanguard of modern Iran.

Madrasah Soltani

Known as the Imam Khomeini School, this 19th century mosque is located next to the Jewelers' Bazaar. It attracts tourists because of its excellent plan and design, vast spaces, double-shell 27-m. high brick dome, and pleasant landscape. Altogether, there are 8 historic inscriptions inside the building. It is open to visitors every day from 8 a.m. to 6 p.m. Masjid-e Jame', Maidan Mosque, and Soltan Amir Ahmad Shrine, are worth to be visited before going to the nearby towns of Natanz and Qamsar and Abyaneh village.

Boroujerdiha Old House

The present premises of Kashan Cultural Heritage Department, the Boroujerdiha Old House was built nearly 130 years ago by a famous merchant and landowner named Haj Seyyed Ja'far Boroujerdi from Natanz, who imported goods from Boroujerd in Lorestan Province. Its completion required 18 years of work by tens of laborers, master painters, and architects. Reception, ceremonial, and residential halls and rooms are arranged on the four sides of the courtyard. Provision of well-proportioned spaces, nicely-designed *bad-girs* (wind-towers) to fit the building, particularly paintings by the famous Iranian painter Kamal-ol Molk Ghaffari, have served to convert it to an art masterpiece in itself.

There are many other old houses in Kashan, such as the Abbassian and Tabatabaei.

Aqa Bozorg Theological School

Aqa Bozorg Mosque and Madrasah Complex in Fazel-e Naraqi street, from the second half of the last century (Qajar period), when the country's architects produced a number of unforgettable masterpieces. The Complex was constructed for congregational prayers as well as preaching and teaching sessions held by Mulla Mahdi Naraqhi II, known as Aqa Bozorg. The vast sanctuary of the mosque is in two floors. The first floor, houses 12 cells on three sides, and the mosque appears at the top floor. The building's past has been documented in 7 historic inscriptions.

The Mausoleum of Shahzadeh Ibrahim

The mausoleum of Shahzadeh Ibrahim, built in (1894 A.D.), belongs to the Qajar period. This structure is highly interesting and attractive for possessing a turquoise tile cupola, lofty minarets, a pleasant courtyard and an iwan decorated with mirror-works and paintings.

The portico and the ceiling of the iwan depict ample paintings of a religious nature on a plaster background. The interior of the mausoleum possesses elaborate mirror-works and its frieze is

decorated with colored, glazed bricks.

The inner door of the mausoleum bears an inscription in which the name of Shahzadeh Ibrahim Ibn-e Soltan Ibn-e Musa Ibn-e Ja'far and that of a certain Seyyed Mahdi Ibn-e Haj Seyyed Hosain Boroujerdi (presumably the endower) can be seen together with the date (1885 A.D.). The person responsible for the founding of the edifice is a certain Khaleh Begum, a citizen of Fin, buried inside the mausoleum, and on whose tombstone some verses have been carved in her praise as the benefactor of the endowment.

Abyaneh

One of the most attractive to visit is in the village of Abyaneh, which was completely Zoroastrian right until the time of the intolerant Safavid Shah Isma'il I in whose reign most of the villagers emigrated to India or to Yazd. Even today their costume, way of life and ancient dialect are still practically unchanged.

Drive for about 42 km to Dehji, along the road to Natanz, south of Kashan; a few km, further on, see a good gravel road to the west, before the Hinjan bridge, where a sign indicates Abyaneh and the magnificent Barzrud valley. Some 25 km along this road, passing Hinjan village, you reach Abyaneh at the bottom of a gorge

dominated by a small Mongol fort. The main street goes right through the remains of the 'Atashkadeh' or temple, open on three sides and with a broken dome.

About 300 m from the Atashkadeh, on the same lane, is an interesting mosque with a probably Safavid entrance and corridor, and next to it, below the present building, another mosque believed to be pre-Seljuq, with an exceptionally beautiful and unusual carved wooden mihrab protected by a sheet of glass.

Natanz

Natanz is small mountain town located forty-nine miles from Kashan. Famed for its bracing climate and fruit orchards.

Jame' Mosque in Natanz with its special architectural and decorative merits, belongs to the 12th century A.D. and its portal inscription bears the date (1304 A.D.).

The constructional style of the northern iwan , together with its lofty arch and interior plaster decorations are remarkable.

The Khaneqah of Sheikh Abd-ol Samad is a domed pyramidal structure famous for its architectural technique, stucco decorations, tile-ornamented mihrab, and wooden sepulchral box. The minaret of Khaneqah possesses beautiful tile-works and an inscription which ends with the date (1324 A.D.).

129-Dome of Imam (Soltani) Madrasah

Amin-od Dowleh Timcheh, Kashan Bazaar

The desert city of Kashan, 162 miles south of Tehran, preserves an architectural unity in its bazaars, gardens, mosques and private dwellings which expresses a traditional communal spirit. Arteries inside traditional bazaars converge at regular intervals, forming large vaulted chambers called timchehs where merchants gather to sell specialized wares. These central spaces are often covered by tiled domes, echoing the drama of light piercing volume and creating pattern found in the mosque or shrine. The nineteenth-century Amin-od Dowleh Timcheh lies inside the Kashan bazaar, and is a meeting place for carpet merchants and buyers.

133- Shah-e Yalan Mausoleum, Kashan bazaar

134-135-Abyaneh Village, near Natanz

136- 137- Jame' Mosque and Khaneqah
(monastery) of Sheikh Abd-ol Samad,
Natanz

Yazd

Capital of Yazd Province, the focal point for bus journeys south and southeast to Bandar Abbas or Kerman and Zahedan, and 677 km. southeast of Tehran, right in the center of Iran and almost entirely surrounded by deserts is the city of Yazd. Situated in a long valley just over 1,215 meters above sea level, and occupying an area of 72,000-sq. km., the town can be reached by road, rail and regular flights from Tehran and major towns. The valley is bounded on the southwest by the extensive Shir Kuh range the highest peak of which is 4,075 meters high; to the northeast rises an isolated massif that is nearly 3,000 meters in height. To the north and east lie the deserts Dasht-e Kevir and Dasht-e Lut. It borders on Isfahan and Kerman provinces to the north and south, respectively.

Modern Yazd is an important manufacturing center with cotton, silk, and wool textile mills; a steel plant, a factory making water purification and filtration equipment; carpet-weaving workshops; and food-processing enterprises. Mines near the city produce iron, lead, uranium, and zinc ore, as well as various minerals. Until the very recent past, the town used to draw its scanty water supply mainly from the Shir Kuh Mountain by means of an elaborates system of *qanats* or underground conduits, some of which are as much as 45 km. long. Inhabitants of Yazd (now over 327,751 according to 1996 census) excel all other Iranians in the making of *qanats*, and the services of the highly skilled *muqannis* or *qanats*-makers of Yazd are often in demand in other parts of the country. In rural areas the water obtained from *qanats* is mainly used for irrigation and production of wheat, barley, cotton, oilseeds, indigo, mulberry trees (for silk worms), fruits, almonds, melons, and vegetables. Yazd sits on the main highway and rail line from Tehran to Kerman, Zahedan, and Bandar Abbas. It is also served by an airport.

Yazd's many historical sites include a Friday mosque, where Muslims gather to worship on Fridays. The mosque was built between the 12th and 15th centuries on the site of a pre-Islamic Zoroastrian fire temple. The Friday Mosque, like so many important mosques, was the focus of a complex of buildings of various periods and styles in various states of conservation. There is no more impressive gateway in Iran than this great soaring 14-century edifice. Crowned by a pair of minarets, the highest in Iran, the portal's façade is decorated from top to bottom in dazzling tile-work, predominantly blue in color. Inside there is a long arcaded court where, behind a deep-set southeast *iwan*, is a sanctuary chamber which, under a squat tiled dome, is exquisitely decorated with faience mosaic: its tall faience mihrab, dated 1365, is one of the finest of its kind in existence.

This Zoroastrain fire temple, called Atashkadeh, is located on a hill in a small garden on the east side of Ayatollah Kashani St. It attracts Zoroastrians from around the world. There are also a couple of paintings here, including one of Zoroaster. Architecturally, there are certain similarities between this fire-temple and those of Indian Zoroastrians. There are plenty of other Zoroastrian sites such as *Qal'eh-ye Asadan* (the Fortress of Lions) in the far northeast of Yazd, Towers of Silence (locally known as *Dakhmeh* or *Qal'eh-ye Khamushan* (about 15 km. to the south-west), and the most important one, Chak Chak, 52 km. to the north.

The city is also home to the 14th-century Vaqt-o Sa'at Mausoleum and library, the 15th-century Mir Chakhmaq, and the 15th-century covered bazaar. Several thousand old houses in the center of the city are topped with high wind-towers (*bad-girs*), a traditional architectural feature of Yazd. The towers, some as high as 6 m. (20 ft.), trap breezes and conduct them downward to rooms at ground level, providing a form of early air conditioning. The University of Yazd (founded in 1988) is also here. According to some historical documents the history of Yazd goes back to the time of Alexander the Great, or one millennium before the emergence of Islam. It became esteemed for its silk textiles during the Sassanian Empire (224-641 A.D.). It was conquered by the Arabs in 642 A.D., and subsequently became an important station on the caravan routes to Central Asia and India, again exporting its silks, textiles and carpets far and wide. It continued to be an important trade and silk center through the 13th century. Because of its relatively remote location, the Mongols, who destroyed many Iranian cities in the 13th century, did not attack Yazd or the area around it. Yazd's prosperity thus was not interrupted, and the city flourished until the 18th century, when it was attacked and looted by the Afghans, who massacred most of Yazd's residents during the course of the 19th century. Yazd gradually recovered from that disaster. As an early focus of industrialization efforts in the 1930s, the city experienced an economic renaissance in the 20th century, until the extension of the railway line here under the last Shah and particularly after the victory of Islamic Revolution.

Yazd represents a microcosm of dilemmas and arts, the troubled social and religious harmonies that invigorate Iran. Zoroastrians have always been populous in Yazd. Even now roughly twelve thousand of the town's population adhere to this ancient religion, and though their fire temple was turned into a mosque when the Arabs invaded Iran, a dignified new fire temple was inaugurated thirteen hundred years later.

There are a good number of other sites around Yazd, and in nearby towns of Na'in and Zavareh.

139- Mir Chakhmaq old gateway, Yazd

Maidan and the Tekiyeh of Mir Chakhmaq

This Maidan and the Tekiyeh, once considered the entrance portal of the old Bazaar of Yazd, belong to the late (15th cent. A.D.), and were founded in (1426 A.D.), when Masjid-e Mir Chakhmaq was also under construction. However, the portal, two high tile-decorated minarets and several of the present arcades date from the (19th cent. A.D.), added during the Qajar period.

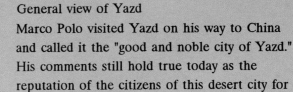

General view of Yazd

Marco Polo visited Yazd on his way to China
and called it the "good and noble city of Yazd."
His comments still hold true today as the
reputation of the citizens of this desert city for
honesty and hard work remains undiminished.
Centered in the heart of Iran between the Kavir
and Lut deserts, Yazd was a major stop on the
international caravan routes to Central Asia and
India. The weavers of Yazd were famous for
their silk brocades which can still be found,
although the traditional weavers are hard
pressed to compete with modern factory cloth.
The architecture of Yazd is perhaps the most
traditionally Persian to be found, preserved by
the hot, dry climate and spared the devastations
of the Mongols. This view from the dome of the
fourteenth-century Friday Mosque shows the
sun-backed roofs and windtoers of the city.

141- 142- Mausoleum of Seyyed Rokn-od Din

Seyyed Rokn-od Din Mausoleum

This Mausoleum belongs to the (14th cent. A.D.) and possesses a portal, a fine cupola covered with enamelled tiles, and an inscription in Kufic calligraphy.

Inside the cupola, there are brick decorations, and the construction of the mausoleum has been attributed to Amir Rokn-od Din Mohammad Qazi. Before becoming a mausoleum, the building was known under the name of Masjid-e Mosalla-ye Atiq.

144- Hammam-e Khan (Khan Bath) , Traditional tea-house, Yazd

◀145- An old passageway, Yazd

146- Rooftop of Abarqu Jame' Mosque near Yazd

148- Silk brocades workshop, Yazd

Jame' Mosque, Ardestan

The drive from Natanz to Ardestan (almost due east) is a dog-leg jaunt of 70 km. with the desert on the left all the way. The present Friday Mosque in Ardestan can be dated late in the twelfth century. It is one of the finest examples of Seljuq architecture in central Iran, in the same style as the Friday Mosques of Isfahan , Zavareh (15 km. north-east of Ardestan) and Golpaigan (between Isfahan and Arak). In Ardestan one marvels at the whirling arabesques on the vault of the iwan.

Na'in

Ninety-six km. beyond Ardestan along a rather bumpy track that keeps veering towards the desert as though eager to lure one away from the lifeline of cities, is the sleepy little town of Na'in.

The Friday Mosque of Na'in, exceptional in that it dates from the period before four iwans had become the norm, in the eleventh (?) century or possibly even earlier if one judges by the elegant stucco reliefs (once polychrome) on arch, mihrab and column.

Jame' Mosque, Na'in

The Jame' of Na'in is one of the famous historic monuments of Iran and its original construction belongs to the (10th cent. A.D.). From the constructional point of view, the crescent-shaped arches of this mosque bear close resemblance to those of the Tarikhaneh mosque of Damghan, and the Jame' of Nairiz in Fars. The monument possesses eleven arcades with semi-circular vaults, the one in the middle being wider than the rest. Upon the walls, the vaults and the pillars, there are various octagonal and other geometric decorations worked in plaster mouldings, particularly worthy of note for their simple charm and deep setting. This last point supports the belief that the monument is one of the early Islamic structures, and a historic relic of considerable artistic value. Upon the minbar, there is an inscription in Naskh style, carved on a floral background and dated 711 A.H. (1311 A.D.), which is the date of the donation, by Jamal-od Din Malek-ol Tojjar, of the minbar. Further, a panel inscription on the door of the mosque, bears the date 874 A.H. (1469) A.D.), which is that of repairs on the monument.

This mosque is also known as the Masjid-e Alavian.

◀149- Ardestan Jame' Mosque

150-153- General view of Zavareh and its Jame' Mosque

175

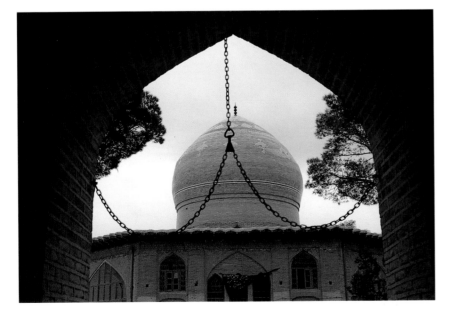

155-159- General views of Na'in (far left) Narang Qal'eh (old fortifications) and Jame' Mosque (right), Na'in wind-towers and cisterns, Mosalla (prayer hall) and bazaar passageway.
160-161, Ardestan Jame' Mosque ►

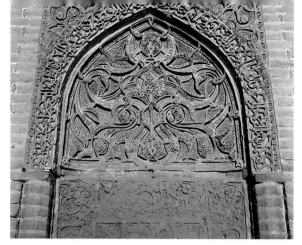

Kerman

The capital of Kerman Province, located in an altitude of 1,860 m. above sea level and 1,062 km. To the south of Tehran, Kerman is a wonderful place. Unless one travels to Kerman by air, it seems a very long way from any other center of importance, no matter whether one approaches it from the northwest, the southwest or the southeast.

The town is situated close to the wastes of Dasht-e Lut, from which it is separated by a range of mountains. Kerman has had a long and turbulent history, and it has only for short spells enjoyed peace and prosperity at the same time. Late in the 18 th century A.D. Aqa Mohammad Khan, Shah of Qajar dynasty, took a terrible vengeance on the people of Kerman because they had given help to his mortal enemy Lotfali Khan Zand. The town has a Zoroastrian minority, altogether much smaller than that in Yazd.

The pistachio is grown principally in the Rafsanjan-Kerman area. Most of the ancient Kerman was destroyed in 1794 earthquake, and the modern Kerman radiates from two squares (Azadi and Shari'ati), and all the monuments of interest lie between these two, and include:

162-163- Hammam-e Vakil (an old bath now used as a tea house), tile-works of hammam-e (bath) Ibrahim Khan

164-165- Portal of Kerman's national library, interior of Malek Mosque

182

166- Tile-works of Malek Mosque

Ganj Ali Khan Bath and Ethnological Museum

The Ganj Ali Khan Bath (*hammam*) is one of the several ancient monuments and a group of utilitarian buildings in Vakil Bazaar dating from the Safavid period in the 17th century. It houses an interesting exhibition of good wax works of men in various poses and costumes set in a traditional but no longer operational bath-house. The Bath, named after a former governor of the province, is being kept as a real hammam, but its life-size wax figures bring back the memory of everyday scenes of the past. All garments and other objects exhibited belong to the same period: razors, sandals, phials for attar of roses, pipes with small bowls and long stems to be enjoyed after the bath.

167-169- Waxed figures and tile-works of Hammam-e Ganj Ali Kahn (an old bath now turned into a museum), Kerman

Vakil Bazaar

The extensive Regent's Bazaar, constructed of beautiful and preserved brick, much of it from the Safavid period, is largely of interest for its architecture rather than for the range of goods, although there are a few metalwork shops selling brass and copper trays and the like noisily hammered into shape on site.

170- Ganj Ali Kahn Square

Bam

The historical Bam, in an altitude of 1000 m., is a half-dead, half-living town 195 km. to the southeast of Kerman. Once a famous citadel and a strategic stronghold, the old Bam has been built on a huge rock mass at the northeast of the living town, and is a city moulded in the red clay of the Great Iranian Desert, Dasht-e Kevir. Locally, it is called "Arg-e Bam" meaning Bam Citadel, 300 m. long and 200 m. wide, consisting of two parts. It is similar to a large medieval European castle, except that the material is not stone but brick. It is surrounded by a more than three-kilometer long crenellated wall supported by dozens of towers for the defense of the town.

171- Coppersmiths bazaar

172- Arg-e Bam (an old fortification)

Mahan

35 km. south of Kerman on the Bam road, Mahan is renowned for the sanctuary of a saintly person said to have lived for a hundred years, from 1331 to 1431: Shah Nur-od Din Ne'matollah Vali, poet, sage, Sufi and founder of Ne'matollahi order of dervishes, who are quite numerous in Iran and meet in the sanctuary of Mahan. They are peaceful people of the Mohammedan faith. To them life means being uprooted; their striving is for the return through death to their "native land, relying on their activities, patience and tolerance"

Bagh-e Shazdeh

Mahan has also an attractive historical garden from the Qajar period, called Bagh-e Tarikhi-e Shazdeh (Prince's Historical Garden). The combination of delightful scenery and the charm of its mausoleum is very restful.

173-174- Mausoleum of Shah Ne'matollah Vali (mystic Sufi)

Southern Iran

Shiraz

A city in southwestern Iran and capital of Fars Province in the Zagros Mountains, Shiraz is a commercial center of the surrounding region, which produces grapes, citrus fruit, cotton, and wheat. The chief products are inlaid articles of wood, metalwork, especially silver, rugs, brocades, and other textiles, cement, electronic parts, and fertilizer. It is the city of historic monuments, poets and philosophers, warriors and kings, orchards, orangeries, roses, adonises and fragrant blossoms. With a population of 973,161 inhabitants, it lies in a pleasant green valley surrounded by high mountains, in the vicinity of Lake Maharlou. Its climate is extremely agreeable and generally temperate because of the city's altitude (1,600 m.). During Now Ruz (the Iranian New Year beginning on 21st March) the city becomes a field of flowers and greenery, heady with scent of orange-blossom. Points of interest in Shiraz include the tombs of the celebrated Persian poets Hafez and Sa'di, both natives of the city, the Khalili Garden, Bagh-e Eram (the Garden of Paradise), Bagh-e Delgosha, Qavam Orangery (Naranjestan-e Qavam), Tekiyeh Haft Tanan, the Koran Gate, Vakil Mosque, Shah Cheragh Shrine, Attiq Friday Mosque, New Mosque (Masjid-e Now), Pars Museum, Bishapur (Ancient ruins, to the west of Shiraz), and Fasa and Firuzabad (Ruins in the surroundings of Shiraz). The city is also the site of a university (1945). Shiraz was founded in the 7th century and was the capital of Iran during several periods of its history.

Hafeziyeh

Hafez (1325?-1389?) is a world-famous Persian poet, who was born here into a poor family Originally named Mohammad Shams-od Din, he gained the respectful title Hafez, meaning "one who has memorized the Koran," as a teacher of the Koran. He was a member of the order of Sufi mystics and also, at times, a court poet. His poems on one level celebrate the pleasures of drinking, hunting, and love at the court of Shiraz. On a deeper level, according to some scholars, they reflect his consuming devotion as a Sufi to union with the divine. They also satirize hypocritical Muslim religious leaders. He was known as having memorized the Holy Koran in 14 versions. Hafez work, collected under the title of *Divan* (trans. 1891), contains more than 500 poems, most of them in the form of a *ghazal*, a short traditional Persian form that he perfected. Each consists of up to 15 highly structured rhyming couplets dealing with one

subject. The language is simple, lyrical, and heartfelt. Hafez is greatly admired both in Iran and, in translation, in the West.

Bagh-e Eram (Garden of Paradise)

A Qashqai tribal chief, Mohammad Qoli Khan Il-khani, built the idyllic Bagh-e Eram in the early eighteenth century, planting it with cypress, pine, orange and persimmon trees, and calling it after the garden of Paradise described symbolically in the Koran. About seventy-five years later, Nasir-al Molk bought the gardens, and constructed this elegant two-story pavilion designed by a famous Shirazi architect, Mohammad Hasan, who was also the architect for Nasir-al Molk's town house in Shiraz. The tiled rooms of the lower floor lie partly underground, and are cooled by a stream of water that flows from the house into a large central pool and down this rose-lined garden promenade.

Naranjestan (Place of Oranges)

One of the best-preserved of the Shiraz houses is the ancestral home of the Qavam family, Naranjestan, which means Place of Oranges, built in the 1870s by Mirza Ibrahim Khan. The Qavam family were originally merchants who came to Shiraz from Qazvin, but soon became active in government serving under the Zand, Qajar and Pahlavi Dynasties. Naranjestan preserves the elegance and refinement enjoyed by upper-class Persian families in the nineteenth century. Living quarters for men, women and guests, working areas, cool gardens and well-equipped kitchens all cohere in this organized Persian household. The mirrored porch was the focal point of the men's quarters and opens onto gardens lined with date palms.

Nasir-ol Molk Mosque

The structure and tile decoration of the Nasir-ol Molk Mosque, completed in 1888, closely resemble the eighteenth-century Vakil Mosque also in Shiraz. Its western prayer hall is enclosed on the courtyard side by stained-glass doors, and is used by the congregation during cold weather. Inside, two rows of six twisted stone columns with acanthus capitals support small tiled domes.

Shah Cheragh Mausoleum

Shah Cheragh was the brother of the Eighth Imam, Reza, whose sacred shrine is at Mashhad. The tomb of this ninth-century martyr draws thousands of pilgrims annually, and is the principal pilgrimage center in the province of Fars, and one of the few Shi'ite shrines accessible to the discreet non-Muslim.

177- Bagh-e Eram, a 19th cent. Garden

197

Vakil Bazaar

Karim Khan Zand (1750-1779) assumed the title of Vakil or Regent and ruled Persia from his capital at Shiraz. One of his major contributions was the building of the large Vakil Bazaar whose main axis cuts north-south across the city and leads into the tiled Vakil Mosque. The Vakil Bazaar was constructed of yellow bricks following the design of the earlier royal bazaar in Isfahan, and is considered by many to be the finest bazaar in Iran.

Pasargadae

The first capital of the Iranian tribes and the Achaemenian empire, Pasargadae is situated between the present-day Marvdasht and Sa'adatabad 130 km. to the northeast of Shiraz, not far from Isfahan-Shiraz road and less than 50 km. from Persepolis. The nearby village is called Madar-e Solaiman (Solomon's Mother) in much the same legendary way as Persepolis is known as Takht-e Jamshid (The Throne of Jamshid). But there is mythology about Cyrus the Great (550-530 B.C.) and his son Cambyses II (530-521 B.C.) who created the military encampment and associated buildings that the visitor now sees, with a clear influence of the Mesopotamian ziggurat.

Persepolis

The center of the great Persian Empire, ceremonial capital of the Achaemenians and the showpiece of Achaemenian art, Persepolis (Capital of Persia, in Greek) is a historic site in Fars Province, 60 km. to the northeast of Shiraz by road, for which the Iranians have got their own name: *Takht-e Jamshid* (The Throne of Jamshid), Jamshid being the first, probably mythical, ruler of Iran. It is 420 km. south of Isfahan and 835 km. south of Tehran on a first-class asphalt road. It can be reached by air through Shiraz international airport. Also called Parsa by the ancient Persians, it was used as a residence by the Achaemenian kings, beginning with Darius I in the late 6th century B.C. The site consists of the remains of several monumental buildings on a vast stone terrace surrounded by a brick wall. The palace and audience hall (Apadana) of Darius I contain sculptured relief depicting Achaemenian court ceremonies. Thirteen of the Apadana's massive stone columns are still standing, and its broad double staircase has been restored by archaeologists. At Naqsh-e Rostam, some 6 km. (about 4 mi.) northwest of Persepolis are the Achaemenian royal tombs. Plundered and burned by Alexander the Great in 330 B. C., Persepolis was eventually abandoned. Excavation of the site began in 1931, supervised by James Henry Breasted of the University of Chicago's Oriental Institute.

178-179- Interior design of Qavam
House or Naranjestan,
a 19th century
residence

180-181- Nasir-ol Molk Mosque, Shiraz

184-185-Vakil Bazaar

187- Bas-relief of delegations, Apadana Palace, Persepolis

188-190- Tomb of Cyrus, Solomon Prison, (top) Madar-e Solaiman platform

191- Tachara Palace, Darius' Palace, Persepolis

192- A Capital, (5th cent. B.C.), Persepolis

Sassanian Bas-reliefs, Tang-e Chogan

On two sides of the surface of the rocky Tang- e Chogan (on the right and left), there are six bas-reliefs, sculptured during the Sassanian period. These include:

1- Victory of Shapur I over Valerian.

2- The same scene with more detail.

3- The actual scene of Valerian's humble submission to Shapur I. This is by far the greatest sculpture of the Sassanian period.

4- Bas-relief of Bahram II.

5- Bas-relief representing the investiture of Bahram I by Ahura Mazda.

6- Shapur victory over his foes.

The tomb of Cyrus I

Tomb of Teisoes or Cyrus I, on the way to Kazeroun near Bushehr, known as Gur-e Dukhtar is the most important building belonging to the Achaemenian era, discovered by Professor Vanden Berghe in 1960, Perhaps this building belonged to one of the ancestors of Cyrus the Great, such as Teispes, or Cyrus I. The last-named king was the grandfather of Cyrus the Great, and according to an inscription of Ashurbanipal in 639 B.C. he was King of Parsuash or Parsa. This tomb, without the smallest doubt, is a pre-example of the tomb of Cyrus.

Bushehr

The capital of Bushehr Province in southwestern Iran and located on the Persian Gulf. Bushehr is a major fishing and commercial port, and an export market for the farm produce of the neighboring and fertile Fars Province. Bushehr's industries include seafood canneries, food-processing plants, and engineering firms. The old section of central Bushehr has many examples of traditional Persian Gulf architecture from the period 1870 to 1920.

Siraf Port

Siraf was a flourishing port on the Persian Gulf during the ninth and tenth centuries A.D., facilitating trade between West Asia, India and Ceylon. Archaeologists have exposed some of the city which stood along a sheltered bay near the village of Taheri, 150 miles southeast of Bushehr. With the discovery of Sassanid remains underlying the Islamic town, Siraf has become one of the few excavated sites that offer a glimpse into that hazy transitional period between the fall of the Sassanid Empire and the introduction of Islam into Persia by the Arabs in the seventh century.

195- Dasht-e Arjan, on the way to Kazeron ▶

196-197- Sassanian bas-reliefs, 7th century, Tang-e Chogan
198- Nature of Bushehr

199- Gur-e Dokhtar (Tomb of Teispes), Cyrus I, (6th cent. B.C.), Kazeroun, southern Fars

200- A View of Siraf, Bandar-e Taheri

Bandar Abbas

Sea-port and capital of Hormozgan Province, Bandar Abbas is located on the south of Iran at sea level and overlooks the strategic Strait of Hormoz. It is a port in the middle of strait linking the Persian Gulf to the Sea of Oman. With a distance of 1,501 km. from Tehran, it can be reached by air, a first-class road, and rail. Compared to other ports along the Persian Gulf and the Sea of Oman, modern Bandar Abbas is the largest and the most equipped port that occupies a strategic position of the greatest importance. In summer it gets sizzling hot and very humid there, but it's pleasant enough to visit in winter.

In the 16th century, the Portuguese took possession of the Isle of Hormoz in order to use the latter as an outpost for the protection of their Indian empire. They were expelled in 1622 after a tough naval battle, by shah Abbas the Great who founded the town that continues to bear his name ever since (it was called Gambro or Gambrun until then). Following the downfall of Safavid dynasty and the Afghan invasion of Iran, Nader Shah became the king of Iran. He expelled the Afghans from Iran and, among other things, constructed a ship building industry and the corresponding port facilities at Bushehr, as the result of which the fame of Bandar Abbas eclipsed and the town began to fall into ruin. Revival of Bandar Abbas took place only recently. Its all- round development has been the result of social, commercial, military, political, and tourism imperatives. Close to the Arab world and, through the Sea of Oman, open to the oceans of Asia, Bandar Abbas is serving Iran as its most natural maritime outlet at present.

The port stretches out along a narrow and long coastal strip. The main east-west thoroughfare changes its name from Shahid Beheshti Blvd. to Imam Khomeini Street and then to Pasdaran Blvd. The main docks (Shahid Ba-honar) are in the west of town, the airport and bus station to the east and the main road out of Bandar Abbas in all directions extends eastwards from Shahid Beheshti Blvd.

A considerable part of the local population lives on the proceeds of its fishing activities. Partly employing the traditional net, most of them are using modern methods of preservation and transport which has led to a rapid extension of Iranian fisheries industry. Industrial fishing is carried out in the Sea of Oman and the Indian Ocean. Agriculture goes on with two annual harvests: early out of season garden products, fruits, dates, and citrus.

During the last three decades, the well-to-do citizens of the capital, as well as some northerners coming, for example, from Tabriz and Mashhad, hit on the bright idea of indulging in winter holidays under the southern sun. At that time of the year the climate is astonishingly mild at Bandar Abbas. The great damp heat does not start before May and becomes unbearable only between June and September. The wide beaches are covered with silky sand, cleansed by fairly ample tides. The gentle slope provides a safe playground for children. The newly constructed hotels offer gardens, swimming pools and playing fields.

201- 207- Views of Bandar Abbas, Kong Port, Hormoz Isle

An interesting local tradition which will be seen in Bandar Abbas and many other coastal towns of Hormozgan Province, are the *borqas* or the owl-like "masks" worn by some women, which are fairly hideous, semi-rigid contraptions surrounding eyes and cheek-bones and covering the nose. The Iranians believe that no religious taboo explains the wearing of these masks: rather it is a fashion which originates from the period of Portuguese occupation when ladies wished to walk about unrecognized or simply to protect their face from the scorching sun.

Many of the men still wear *aba* (a long, sleeveless, usually white robe), sandals or flip-flops and sometimes a turban. The traditional Bandari dress is most common in Hormozgan province, especially on the islands.

Southwestern Iran

Khuzestan

The area covers southern Iran from Khorramshahr and Abadan in the southwestern to Bandar Abbas in the southern Iran. The three coastal provinces - Hormozgan, Bushehr, and Khuzestan - are hot and humid all year round. The only truly pleasant time to visit them is November to March.

Abadan and Khorramshahr which were among big industrial and commercial centers of Iran due to oil explorations as from early 20th century, are now under total reconstruction after Iran-Iraq War. At present the center of activity has shifted to the Province of Hormozgan, mainly around Bandar Abbas, in Kish and Qeshm Islands out of 14 large, inhabited and interesting Iranian islands.

The indigenous people of the Iranian shores of the Persian Gulf are often loosely known as Bandaris, from the Persian word of *bandar* for port. Of Arab, Negro, or mixed stock, the Bandaris are darker skinned than the Persians.

Because of the excessive heat in the Persian Gulf region, the siesta is taken very seriously here, even in winter, and very little except public transport functions between noon and late afternoon. Offices and shops close throughout the afternoon and reopen for a few hours at about 5 or 6 p.m.

Despite being largely desert, semi-desert or mountainous, limes and other citrus fruits, cotton, tobacco, and dates are grown in the region. There are more than 200 varieties of fish, among other marine life, in the Persian Gulf, but there are surprisingly little variety in the markets and restaurants, although excellent shrimps and prawns are widely available.

Elam kingdom of ancient Asia, situated north of the Persian Gulf and east of the Tigris River, actually occupied an area corresponding approximately to the present –day Province of Khuzestan. The capital of Elam was Susa, today the city of Shush. Other leading cities included Awan, Simash, Madaktu, and Dur Untash, the site of present-day Chogha Zanbil ziggurat.

Imamzadeh Abdollah (Abdollah Mausoleum), Shushtar

The present structure of the Mausoleum, where the date 629 A.H. (1231 A.D.) can be read, belongs to the (13th cent. A.D.).

This mausoleum stands on a hillock in the southern part of the town, inside an enclosure. A Kufic portal inscription in the mausoleum, contains the date: "Muharram of the year 629 (1231 A.D.)" The mausoleum appears to have had other appurtenances, such as a Madrasah, library and inn, all of which have now disappeared.

209-210- Abdollah Mausoleum and its old prayer niche

The ancient city of Shush (Susa)

The ancient city of Shush (Susa), capital of Elam, was an important and flourishing city before the advent of Islam. Scientific excavations begun in 1891 A.D. by French archaeological missions, and continued until the present time, have brought to light many remains and relics of a pre-historic civilization. For instance copper objects and utensils discovered in the lowest stratum have resulted in ascribing this layer to the Copper Age, while the existence of yellow colored earthenware, decorated with animal motifs and geometric designs have evidenced the existence of a pottery-making industry in Iran, some 3000 to 2500 years before Christ.

In the second stratum of this Elamite city, a great number of objects made of stone, copper and other metals, and some cylinders made of bone have been discovered, while the higher strata have revealed kiln-fired, colored and decorated earthenware, metal arms, cylinders, copper pins, as well as human and animal figures.

The historic site of Susa is divided into four sections in respect to their antiquity and archaeological importance.

In all these sections, ample relics including pottery, arms, ornamental objects, metalwork, bronze articles, as well as tablets bearing traces of pictographic writing have been discovered. Similarly, numerous clay and stone tablets have been unearthed in Susa, which date back to 1700 B.C. The texts of these tablets are usually of documentary, legal or contractual nature.

The Ziggurat of Chogha Zanbil, Susa, Khuzestan

The Elamite temple of Chogha Zanbil is located on a high mound on the bank of the river Dez, a tributary of the Karun, and was built in 1250 B.C. by the Elamite king Untash Gal for the Elamite deity "Inshushinak". It is about 25 meters high and consists of several storeys, made of mud brick and revered with kiln-fired bricks. A number of clay tablets and human and animal statuettes have been discovered around the temple.

During excavations in the mound, two bricks inscribed in Elamite script were discovered.

The Ziggurat has a quadrangular base and its original height is believed to have been about 50 meters, the highest storey of the structure belonging to Inshushinak. The splendid portals and numerous stairways of the monument have been constructed in such a way as to lead, one and all, to the upper storeys.

211- Tile-works of Susa Palace

◀212- 213- The ancient city of Susa and Chogha Zanbil Ziggurat, 1250 B.C.

Tomb of Ya'qub Ibn-e Layth Saffari

Ya'qub Ibn-e Layth was the founder of the Safavid Dynasty whose center was in Sistan. This popular hero valiantly challenged the powerful Arab Caliphate, and expanded his rule across Fars as far as Khuzestan where he died at Jondishapur in A.D. 879. His impressive tomb stands on the edge of a small village and is being restored.